THE CAROLINA WATERMEN

OTHER BOOKS BY RICHARD KELLY

V. S. Naipaul
Graham Greene
The Andy Griffith Show
The Best of Mr. Punch: The Humorous Writings of Douglas Jerrold (ed.)

Twayne English Authors Series:

Graham Greene: A Study of the Short Fiction
Lewis Carroll
Daphne du Maurier
George du Maurier
Douglas Jerrold

THE CAROLINA WATERMEN
Bug Hunters and Boatbuilders

Richard Kelly

and

Barbara Kelly

JOHN F. BLAIR, PUBLISHER   WINSTON-SALEM, NORTH CAROLINA

Book Design by Debra Long Hampton
Printed and Bound by Quebecor America Book Group
Printed on acid-free paper

Library of Congress Cataloging-in-Publication Data

Kelly, Richard Michael, 1937–
The Carolina watermen :
bug hunters and boatbuilders / Richard and Barbara Kelly.
p.   cm.
Includes index.
ISBN 0-89587-104-1
1. Holden Beach (N.C.) — Social life and customs.   2. Holden Beach
(N.C.) — Biography.   3. Shrimpers (Persons) — North Carolina — Holden
Beach — Biography.   4. Shrimp fisheries — North Carolina — Holden Beach —
History.   I. Kelly, Barbara, 1938– .   II. Title.
F264.H78K45   1994
975.6'29 — dc20   93–17464

IN MEMORY OF

Edna Nicholson

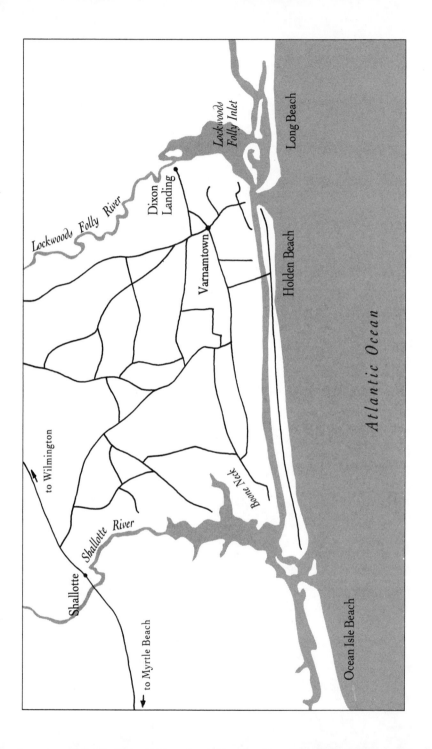

CONTENTS

ACKNOWLEDGMENTS

This book could not have been written without the generous, indeed joyful, cooperation of the many people we interviewed. We are especially grateful to Pete Singletary, who first directed us to Goodman Fulford, Weston Varnam, and Norman Bellamy. Those people, in turn, introduced us to many of the other people who comprise the heart of this book. We were invited into the homes and onto the boats of some of the most gracious people in Brunswick County. We hope that this small book may be received by them as a token of our affection. Given the storm warnings of social, economic, and environmental change, we also hope that this book will bear testimony to the fundamental decency, hard work, and creative energy of an endangered species, the Carolina waterman.

We would also like to thank Marjorie Macgivern for supplying us with some essential material about the history of shrimping; Rich Carpenter and Paul Phalen of the North Carolina Division of Marine Fisheries for answering several of our questions about shrimp and shrimp landings in Brunswick County; the *Brunswick Beacon* for allowing us to examine their files for a variety of historical information; and Judy Bryan for her photographs in the chapter on the loggerhead turtles.

Finally, we would like to thank the people at John F. Blair, Publisher, for their enthusiastic support of our project from its conception.

INTRODUCTION

We first visited Holden Beach, North Carolina, in September of 1983. Located midway between Wilmington, North Carolina, to the north and Myrtle Beach, South Carolina, to the south, Holden Beach is a narrow island almost eleven miles in length that has long been popular with families wanting to escape from the condominiums and commercial clutter of other area resorts. Having driven over four hundred miles from Knoxville, Tennessee, we eagerly approached the sea as we drove over a small, rickety drawbridge spanning the Intracoastal Waterway and headed down the island towards our rental house. Only one road runs the east-west length of the island, and the nearly unbroken row of beachfront houses and tall sand dunes made it impossible to glimpse the ocean. We rolled down the car windows to sniff and hear the ocean but smelled nothing and heard only a few sea gulls.

Upon entering the house, we drew the blinds and opened the door leading to the beach and were quietly startled to see the expanse of ocean and soft, white sand that up to this time had been so successfully hidden away. Holden Beach, at last! Only a handful of people were visible along the length of the sand. Here was an unusual beach, where the sandpipers, gulls, and brown pelicans clearly outnumbered the visitors and graced the seascape with their flight and beauty.

Holden Beach soon became a state of mind for us, a dream place to remember during the rest of the year and to look forward to revisiting. And so, over the ensuing years, we have returned to Holden Beach each fall. We have seen many changes on the island. The small drawbridge over the Waterway was replaced by a white concrete high-rise bridge that allows the tallest boats to easily pass under it. Although the new bridge is out of scale with the rest of the landscape, it affords an astonishing first view of the ocean and the entire length of the island. The number of beachfront and second-row houses has increased; they now extend to the private western tip of the island. There are also more second-row houses, obstructing the view of the marshes along the Intracoastal Waterway.

Perhaps the most significant change to Holden Beach, however, has been wrought not by realtors and builders but by nature itself. In only a few years, the winter storms and especially Hurricane Hugo have reshaped the island. The lashing winds and powerful high tides wrought by Hugo destroyed several houses, half of the Holden Beach pier, and all of the wooden walkways leading from the houses to the beach. They also swept away some twenty to thirty feet of beachfront. Much of the soft, white sand that sheltered ghost crabs and provided a seemingly endless supply of building material for children's fantasies has been replaced with hard-packed sand under the constant high tides that now lap around the supports of hundreds of rebuilt wooden steps leading from the houses to the beach.

In years past, when the only buildings along the beach were a few small fisherman's shacks and modest cottages, the powerful storms and erosion could easily be accommodated. Now, however, with millions of dollars in real estate poised dangerously along the edge of the ocean, an expensive and perhaps futile struggle between landowners and nature has begun.

While looking out on the unchanging ocean over the years from the comfortable perspective of a beachfront porch, we began wondering about the soul of this small island, the dynamic and unseen force that gave it life long before the vacationers arrived and continues to sustain it long after they have all gone home. We watched the hypnotic waves for hours as shrimp boats, barely visible in the mist, glided as if in a dream, their outriggers extended like the slender arms of a ballerina dancing upon the waters. At first, these forms merely occupied our peripheral vision, but gradually, these mysterious boats became part of our dream place. Their distant presence endowed them with a romance that distracted us from the realities of erosion, storms, pollution, and greedy land developers. Even at night, when the sky and ocean were black, the lights from these invisible boats suggested mysteries. We wondered what was going on in those small cabins of light miles away from shore. During the day, we focused our binoculars on those elusive boats, hoping to catch a glimpse of their ghostly inhabitants, but no one ever materialized.

Perhaps it was they, the mysterious riders of the sea, who comprised the rightful soul of this place. Before the tourists arrived and the expensive houses were strung along the beachfront, these Carolina watermen were building magnificent boats and working the sea. We eventually discovered, however, that their unique way of life, despite its long history and rich traditions, is quickly fading into history. The family of superb craftsmen is no longer building its shrimp boats, and the livelihood of shrimpers and other watermen is now as threatened as the beaches and fine houses that stand on the edge of a storm.

One day at Captain Pete Singletary's seafood house, under the Holden Beach bridge, we saw Pete's shrimp boat, *Amor*, docked outside. Here was one of the ghost ships we could actually touch. The palpable smell of diesel fuel and shrimp made the boat a reality for us. Like most people, we assumed shrimp, the most popular seafood in America, were somehow born out of the piles of ice seductively arranged in the seafood displays of Kroger and Food Lion stores, but here were hundreds of pounds of shrimp being hauled out of a boat before our very eyes. We began to wonder, Where did a handsome, eighty-foot-long wooden boat like this one come from? Where does it go? How does the captain locate and collect tons of shrimp from such a vast ocean? Who are the boatbuilders, and who are the men who silently ride the boats miles offshore as vacationers play in the waves and eat the fruits of the sea? Will the graceful white boats be a permanent part of the seascape for future generations to see? Perhaps here, in the bone and sinew and in the history and ingenuity of the Carolina watermen, may be found the soul of this place.

We decided to dedicate our vacations at Holden Beach to answering these questions by chronicling the stories of several Carolina watermen: owners of fish houses and marinas, shrimp-boat captains and workers, and boatbuilders. Their contribution to American culture has been overlooked by most historians, guidebooks, and local histories. Upon discovering that the boatbuilders around Holden Beach, who constructed many of the shrimp boats on the southeast coast, had ceased building boats in the early 1980s and were now in their seventies or eighties, we realized how imperative it was that we begin chronicling their history at once.

Pete Singletary put us in touch with several watermen in the area, and we began our series of interviews with some of the most dedicated, self-effacing, and hard-working people we have ever met. Most of the people we talked to come from families that have lived in the areas for several generations, such as the Galloways, Fulfords, and Varnams. They all have long memories and tell of good times and bad, and most agree that the halcyon days are over. The boatbuilders we spoke with — the Varnam family and Norman Bellamy — are master craftsmen whose inherited genius for turning cypress and pine into magnificent white boats enabled an entire new livelihood to arise in the area. They, too, have long memories and express a profound skepticism about the future of commercial shrimping in the area.

Commercial fisherman and author William McCloskey

observes that "with man's other sources of animal food neatly domesticated, fishermen have become the last of the hunters." He goes on to characterize the complexity of their enterprise:

> No single account of men and women who fish for a living can tell their entire story. They fish by themselves and collectively, in oceans and estuaries warm and cold during all seasons, in every manageable sea state from calm to roaring, wherever the waters support edible marine life. They cast from shore, they pull nets and lines by hand from open skiffs under oar, balancing themselves inches from the water on slippery thwarts; they labor aboard old gurry buckets that house little more than an engine, a single-burner stove, and tight bunks curved along the inside of the bow; and they work big nets and traps from boats spacious enough to have a separate galley and head, and sometimes even private cabins and a washing machine.[1]

The small commercial shrimpers are certainly among the last of the hunters. They and the people who support their enterprise — the boatbuilders and the owners of fish houses — are quickly receding into history under the pressure of government regulations, environmental problems, the growth of the aquaculture industry, rising costs of fuel and insurance, and the incursion of sportfishing. Despite the death of the boatbuilding business in the area, the shrimpers continue to maintain their boats and drag the ocean bottom for the

---

[1]William McCloskey, *Fish Decks* (New York: Paragon House, 1990), 20.

offspring of the shrimp that supported their fathers and their grandfathers.

In the following pages, we shall sketch a brief history of Holden Beach and then narrate the story of boatbuilding and shrimping based upon the interviews we conducted with various watermen in the area. Although some details might be different, the work and concerns of these men and women are not unlike those of watermen along the coasts of South Carolina, Florida, and the Gulf States. Their knowledge and wisdom are derived from long years of experience and from the rich heritage of their parents and grandparents. What they may fail to express in words has already been written deeply into the soul of maritime history through the hundreds of boats they have built and the thousands of acres of sea they have explored and mined over the decades.

The time we have spent with these people has taught us that the shrimp boat is more than a quaint, picturesque figure in the mist or in a drawing on a restaurant menu. It is the living embodiment of a people and its culture. These people and their lifestyle are now seriously threatened with extinction.

HOLDEN BEACH

Brown pelican overseeing the Intracoastal Waterway

*A*long the coast of Brunswick County, North Carolina, are some of the finest beaches and fresh seafood in the state. Calabash, the self-proclaimed "Seafood Capital of the World," lies in the county's southwest corner, near the South Carolina state line. Heading east, one passes Sunset Beach, Ocean Isle Beach, Holden Beach, Long Beach,

Yaupon Beach, and Caswell Beach, all of which face south towards the Atlantic. Most of these beaches were originally connected to the mainland, but between 1930 and 1931, the United States Army Corps of Engineers dredged the Intracoastal Waterway from Lockwoods Folly Inlet to the South Carolina line, requiring the beach communities to employ ferries and later to construct bridges in order to reach the mainland. Over the years, each island community developed its own character, shaped especially by commercial fishing and later by massive real-estate development, to accommodate vacationers and those wealthy enough to purchase their own piece of the beachfront.

A visitor to these islands today comes to enjoy the sand, surf, seafood, boating, tennis, and golf. The islands are covered with beachfront, second-row, and canal homes, many costing more than $300,000 and built on lots costing well over $200,000. During the past ten years, there have sprung up near the beaches numerous "plantation" communities, featuring expensive retirement homes built around manicured golf courses. In local restaurants, one sees crowds of people dressed in designer golf and tennis outfits discussing their putting and backswings.

In 1950, a developer bought most of Ocean Isle, subdivided the island into tracts of land for sale, and built concrete-walled finger canals along its length. His children then arranged the construction of the county's first high-rise condominiums, two fifteen-story buildings on the island's private west end that can be seen miles away. Ocean Isle also provides a private airport to lure executives down for a weekend of golf.

The Holden Beach area, however, holds a unique place among these islands both in terms of its development and its reputation as a quiet, family-oriented vacation spot. Outside of a miniature-golf establishment, a seafood house, several realty offices, and a few small grocery stores, there is no commercial development on the island. Strict zoning laws restrict the height of buildings to a maximum of thirty-five feet. Practically all of the beachfront property, however, is built up with homes, and now much of the land facing the marshes and the Intracoastal Waterway has also been covered with new homes. Yet there are still remnants of the rough and simple lifestyle of earlier years: small fishing shacks; a few ramshackle, salt-gray cottages tucked in between the large, expensive new homes; the dry dock in nearby Varnamtown; and the remains of several boatbuilding establishments.

The character of the Holden Beach area has been shaped by many forces: by the John Holden family, which first developed the land; by powerful winter storms and hurricanes that stole its sands and destroyed its homes; by the fishermen, shrimpers, and managers of fish houses who made the area noted for its seafood; and by the talented craftsmen who constructed the hundreds of shrimp and fishing boats that work the coast from North Carolina to Florida.

Practically uninhabited until the mid-1930s, the area now known as Holden Beach was first acquired by Benjamin Holden in 1756 as part of a land purchase that extended his plantation to the ocean.[1] At a cost of fifty shillings, he thereby acquired a hundred acres reaching from Lockwoods Folly Inlet

---

[1] Details of the early history of Holden Beach are drawn from John F. Holden's *Holden Beach History* (Wilmington, N. C.: New Hanover Printing and Publishing Co., 1988).

to Bacon Inlet. Upon his death, he bequeathed the eastern half of the beach to one son and the western half to another son. A third son, named Job, managed to buy all the land from his brothers and pass it on to his son, John, and later to his grandson, John Holden, Jr.

John Holden, Jr., was the first to view his land with an entrepreneurial eye towards the future. In 1924, he had a subdivision map made of the area. Two years later, he saw to the construction of the first building on the island, the "Old Hotel," a ten-bedroom guest house built on pilings. During this time, John Holden also established a commercial beach fishery near Lockwoods Folly Inlet. Employing boats, nets, baskets, and barrels, a crew of eighteen men hauled literally tons of mullets and spots onto the beach during the 1920s and 1930s.

Upon the death of John Holden, Jr., his son, Luther, who was living in the nearby town of Bolivia, took over the family property in 1935. He focused his efforts on making Holden Beach into a thriving resort area. He began selling oceanfront lots and building homes to sell and rent at what was now called Holden's Beach Resort.

The war years, however, slowed down his plans to develop the island. Blackouts were enforced each evening. The few vacationers who came for the summer had to close the curtains in their cottages at night, which made the rooms uncomfortably hot, and the local fishermen had to shield from ocean view whatever light they used during their evening work. The United States Coast Guard maintained horse patrols along the beach both to enforce the blackouts and to ensure that German submarines did not compromise the security of the area.

Although Luther Holden lived until 1958, his son, John F. Holden, began to take over the family business in the late 1930s. In 1939, John built the first pavilion with the assistance of three local carpenters. At that time, there were only a total of fifteen cottages on the beach. The vacationers would visit the pavilion during the evening and enjoy square dancing and playing the jukebox for a nickel a song. Luther and his son provided mail service, message delivery, trash pickup, and guided sightseeing tours — at no cost.

Over the ensuing years, John F. Holden has continued to develop the area's reputation as a family beach and to establish the vigorous real-estate business that dominates the island to this day. During his tenure, he has seen several major developments: new roads to and on the island; the construction of the Intracoastal Waterway; the replacement of the ferry to the island by a drawbridge and finally by a high-rise bridge; and the development of boatbuilding, shrimping, and fishing industries.

John F. Holden's influence, however, clearly derives from his careful manipulation of the island's real estate. A large percentage of the homes and land for sale and rent is under the management of his family's business. With precious little land left to develop at this point, he and a few other realtors maintain a profitable rental business that accommodates thousands of visitors each year. The number of cottages on the island rose from 15 in 1939 to 300 in 1954. In 1980, there were slightly over 1,000 housing units, and in 1990, there were over 1,700. Construction of new homes continues. The number of permanent residents on the island increased 170 percent between 1980 and

1990, from 232 to 628. That number is expected to double by the year 2005.

With new beach houses and lots now costing in the range of $200,000 to $400,000 and rentals going for over $1,200 a week, the island is increasingly becoming the province of investors and upper-middle-class summer visitors. Ford and Chevy pickup trucks are everywhere present on the mainland, but it is not unusual to see a Mercedes, a BMW, or a new Dodge Caravan parked between the pilings of an island house. The local marina, on the mainland side of the Intracoastal Waterway, and Capt'n Pete's Seafood House now cater to the changing clientele by offering fishing excursions under the direction of experienced watermen.

Although John F. Holden boasts in his 1988 *Holden Beach History* that the town of Holden Beach "is the only incorporated

Holden Beach, left, as seen from the
Intracoastal Waterway

beach town in Brunswick County that does not have an A. B. C. store, liquor by the drink, beer sales, or night clubs," one may now purchase wine or beer on the island in the same grocery and general stores that sell copies of his book. It is, indeed, still a family beach, but the upper-middle-class families that come to the beach had simply been buying their accustomed beer and wine elsewhere until it was made available on the island.

Even as the Holden family was developing the economic structure and the character of Holden Beach, nature was busy shaping the physical contours of the island according to designs of her own. The two forces were and still are clearly at odds with one another. Over long periods of time, wind and tides build, erode, and rebuild the beaches. Much of the sand on this summer's beach will by next year be carried up or down to another beach or out to sea. Tons of sand are in constant motion. Littoral drift can move sand as much as a mile in one day, and several thousand tons of sand may move past a particular spot in that same period. On a stable beach, the quantity of sand remains constant. The sand that is lost to littoral drift is replaced by sand flowing from up-current islands or by seasonal reversal in wave direction. The natural flow of sand not only makes the beaches continuously erode and build up, but also causes entire islands to move. Most of the barrier islands along the Atlantic coast are migrating southward. North Carolina's Outer Banks, for example, are moving south and west simultaneously.

This littoral drift of sand has been going on for centuries. Only in recent history has it become a problem due to massive real-estate development of the coast. In an attempt to interrupt the natural drift of sand, engineers have tried everything from sea walls to banks of sandbags, but their intervention has had little lasting effect. At Holden Beach, for example, property owners had bulkheads constructed to protect their homes, and the town hired an engineering company to install a battery of nylon-bag groins — large bags filled with cement — to stabilize the vanishing east end of the island. These efforts have not only created one of the ugliest sights on the island, but they do not seem to be working. The east end continues to erode: huge chunks of asphalt and twisted iron supports from the washed-out road lie in heaps; many of the nylon bags have broken open, spilling their contents into the sea; and most of the bulwarks have been destroyed by storms, leaving several houses standing precariously over the water during high tide.

In 1985, the North Carolina Coastal Resources Commission banned sea walls, bulkheads, jetties, and groins. It concluded that such structures may control erosion in one place but hasten it in another, causing the beach to harden. The commissioners, however, responding to the pressure of landowners, are considering a proposal that would simplify the process of asking for an exception to the ban. Believing the restrictions are too strict, several commissioners have recently argued that sea walls, jetties, and groins be allowed on the beach if they would not "cause significant adverse impact" or if they would "provide overriding public benefit."[2]

Besides the littoral drift and the winter storms that play

---

[2]The *Brunswick Beacon* (August 1, 1991), 9a.

constant havoc with the island's store of sand, the two most destructive visitors to Holden Beach were Hurricane Hazel in 1954 and Hurricane Hugo in 1989.

Hurricane Hazel made landfall in the Holden Beach area on October 15, 1954. With winds in excess of 150 miles an hour, Hazel struck the area during high tide and a full moon. Only a handful of the three hundred cottages on the island remained intact after the storm. Nearly seventy feet of oceanfront property running the length of the island were swallowed up in the ferocious tides. Cautious shrimpers who had anchored their boats up Lockwoods Folly River the day before the hurricane managed to save their vessels. The boats left tied to the fish-house docks, however, were driven by the wind and waves into the adjoining woods and suffered major damage.

The storm left at least two people dead, toppled most of the island's electric poles, destroyed most of the six miles of paved road, and rather dramatically opened a new inlet from the Intracoastal Waterway to the Atlantic. The tide rose and fell through this inlet, which now divided the island. Within a year, however, federal funds enabled workmen to close the inlet, and the natural processes of waves and wind slowly restored a portion of the sand that had been carried off to sea.

Nevertheless, property owners, chastened by the devastation, were slow to rebuild, and investors waited several years before gathering up the courage to purchase property on the island. Their caution was twice reinforced: first in September of 1956, when Hurricane Flossy blew some beach cottages off their foundations, and then in September of 1958, when Hurricane Helene, though remaining at sea, set up winds of 135 miles an hour in the area. These two storms were painful reminders of the greater devastation wrought by Hurricane Hazel only a few years earlier. It was not until 1964 that the number of houses on the island finally equaled the total that existed before the arrival of Hazel.

The next twenty years were good ones on the island. Visitors poured in, beachfront houses were built along the length of the island, canal homes were developed along the Intracoastal Waterway, second-row houses lined Ocean Boulevard, and the value of homes and property steadily rose. Despite the indirect effects of subsequent hurricanes and the direct impact of winter storms, the demand for beach property continued to grow. The rich new houses, built on piers and defended by dunes secured with sea oats, grass, and morning glories, seemed impregnable to the vagaries of weather.

As the island was growing affluent with a new generation of realtors, property owners, and vacationers, in the shadowy distance nature was shaping a dark visitor to remind them of the fragility of their enterprise. On the morning of September 22, 1989, Hurricane Hugo, the most destructive tropical storm in history in terms of property damage, made landfall in Charleston, South Carolina, about 135 miles south of Holden Beach. The great size of this storm enabled it to reach north into the Brunswick County coast, causing an estimated $90 million in property damage.

Long Beach, Holden Beach, and Ocean Isle Beach were especially hard-hit. The storm surge flattened the dunes along the entire length of Holden Beach, and walls of water crashed into beachfront homes, toppling some of them off their foundations. With the exception of a few houses on the west end of the island, all of the wooden walkways leading from the houses across the dunes were destroyed, along with the Holden Beach fishing pier. The storm also carried away tons of sand from the beachfront, leaving the houses another twenty to thirty feet closer to the sea.

The town of Holden Beach spent $350,000 to have trucks haul in tons of sand to rebuild the dunes washed away from in front of the houses. Beach grass was planted in these manufactured dunes, and they were further stabilized by a storm fence running the length of the island. Despite financial aid from the state, property owners were assessed a 3-percent tax increase to help pay for the cleanup and repairs.

Dredged from the Intracoastal Waterway, the sand of the

Causeway connecting Holden Beach to the mainland

rebuilt dunes is much coarser than that of the natural dunes. The ghost crabs that riddled the old, soft dunes with their tunnels were slow to inhabit these new structures. Strands of planted grass appear to have taken root, but little natural vegetation has grown out of the new dunes. To make matters worse, the normal winter storms and high tides continue to destroy many of the dunes, along with the storm fence and beach grass, from the middle of the island to its east end. By 1993, almost half of the manufactured dunes had been seriously eroded.

Beaches are ever-changing creatures that can be enjoyed despite the folly that attends them. Beyond the shoulder-to-shoulder beachfront houses and the increasing erosion, one can still see the brown pelicans gliding in formation over the visual wreckage on their way to dinner, the sandpipers pecking their way along the water's edge, the sea roaches burrowing into the soft, wet sand after each wave brings them to shore, and the black skimmers riding the surface of the water and scooping up sparkling fish in their bills.

An array of ropes, nets, and floats

SHRIMPING

Fishing is probably the earliest form of hunting, and, as men were surely hunters before they were cultivators, is actually the oldest industry in the world.

Encyclopedia Britannica, 1954 edition

*S*hrimp may be found in more of the world's waters than any other edible sea creature. They provide a living for fishermen from the warm waters off India and South America to the frigid waters off Norway, Labrador, and Alaska. Although imported shrimp are becoming more and more common in the United States, most Americans still fancy the idea that they are eating the large, succulent shrimp caught in the Gulf of Mexico and along the southeastern coast of the United States.

The greatest volume of shrimp caught in the United States comes from the Gulf of Mexico, where large, steel-hulled shrimp boats go to sea for a month at a time, dragging their nets night and day. These huge boats are actually more like factories than fishing vessels. They not only haul in tons of shrimp, but also process them at sea. The shrimp are deheaded, cleaned, sorted, and packed in ice, ready for market by the time the boat returns to shore.

Most of the shrimping along the coast of the southeastern United States, however, is done by small commercial fishermen working out of wooden boats built ten, twenty, or thirty years ago. They go to sea for only two or three days at a time, return to sell their catch, and then lay off for several days, repairing the nets and maintaining the boats. The fishermen in the Holden Beach area do most of their shrimping during the summer and early fall in the area between Wilmington, North Carolina, and Georgetown, South Carolina. After that, when the water begins to cool, many of the shrimpers work their way farther south, winding up off the coast of Florida by Christmas time.

The size of the catch varies from day to day and from season to season. During the late summer, a good catch consists of ten to fourteen boxes of deheaded shrimp—about a thousand to fourteen hundred pounds—during a four-day outing. In September 1990, the market rate paid to shrimpers was $3.15

a pound, tail weight. If a boat brought in twelve hundred pounds after four days of fishing, the captain would receive $3,780. That amounts to $945 a working day. Out of that sum, he would have to pay his two crew members and pay for his fuel and the cost of maintaining his boat. When shrimping is poor, he is lucky to break even. A man who owns his own boat may make a comfortable living by shrimping here, but he is never going to get rich.

The Shrimp

The shrimp belongs to the class of animal life called Crustacea. The larger crustaceans include the lobster, crayfish, shrimp, and barnacle. The smaller crustaceans include plankton, sow bugs, wood lice, and beach fleas. There are over twenty-five thousand species of crustaceans, most of which live in the sea, where they play a major role in the food chain, keeping the oceans alive. Given its rather grotesque, insectlike appearance —

A tidy arrangement of ropes and doors

beady black eyes, long feelers twitching from its head, ten jointed legs on its thorax and swimmerets on its abdomen, hard carapace — it is a wonder that it has become America's favorite seafood. Of course, most people do not have to experience the ordeal of facing a whole shrimp. They are accustomed to dining on white, breaded, anonymous semicircles of pure flesh.

The two most common species caught by local fishermen off the coast of North Carolina and South Carolina are white shrimp (*Penaeus setiferus*) and brown shrimp (*Penaeus aztecus*). Two other kinds of shrimp are pink shrimp and rock shrimp. Pink shrimp are a variety of brown shrimp, and rock shrimp, which have a hard, thick shell, can only be caught fifty or sixty miles offshore. More abundant in Florida, rock shrimp are not an important part of the Carolina fisherman's catch.

Swimming backwards, both juvenile and adult shrimp feed on any and all organic matter they can find at the bottom of the ocean. Shrimpers have to adjust their fishing to the feeding habits of the particular species. Since white shrimp tend to feed during the day and brown shrimp during the night, one may see trawlers dragging their nets around the clock. In order to conserve the shrimp population, some states, such as South Carolina, have banned night fishing. It is allowed, however, in North Carolina.

The life cycle of the shrimp is something of a mystery. Different marine biologists and different shrimpers tell different stories. Danny Galloway, who has been shrimping out of the Holden Beach area for over two decades, says that his experience confirms what the state biologist has discovered. The adult brown shrimp go into the ocean during the winter, probably in seventy or eighty feet of water, and spawn there. The microscopic spawn then move into the river and rest among the marsh grass. During their development, several factors, such as rainfall and water temperature, affect their growth and health. When they develop to a certain size, they return to the sea, and the shrimpers begin catching them.

The brown shrimp is a burrower and in many areas is more active in open water at night than in the daytime. Like white shrimp, brown shrimp prefer a muddy substrate. In the Carolinas, the landings of brown shrimp outnumber those of white shrimp by two or three to one. The species has a range extending from New Jersey through the Gulf of Mexico and the West Indies to Uruguay, usually at a depth from the water's edge to forty-five fathoms.[1]

White shrimp can be found in the inlets, in the Cape Fear River, and up and down the waters that run the length of the beaches. Their spawning probably begins in May and extends into September. Although white shrimp in Texas may have two spawning periods — spring and fall — those in the Carolinas have only one. A large female shrimp is estimated to produce a half-million to a million eggs at a single spawning. Despite much study, marine biologists have been unable to pinpoint the exact location of the spawning grounds for these shrimp. From the spawning place at sea, a great number of larvae move inshore about two to three weeks after hatching and enter estuaries when they are about seven millimeters long. Once in the

[1] Details of this and other shrimp species are drawn from Austin Williams's *Marine Decapod Crustaceans of the Carolinas* (U. S. Department of the Interior, Fish and Wildlife Service Bureau of Commercial Fisheries, 1965), 18–27.

estuaries on the nursery grounds, the young grow rapidly, increasing in length by about thirty-six millimeters a month. The young, which began by moving from the sea bottom to the fresher, shallower portions of estuaries, move gradually into deeper, saltier water as they grow, and with approaching maturity they return to the sea.

In the fall and winter, shrimp tend to move south along the Atlantic coast. In late winter and early spring, they return north. During the late spring and summer, however, the location of the population is relatively static. The longest recorded southward movement was by a shrimp tagged at Beaufort, North Carolina, in October and recovered 95 days later off Florida, 360 miles from the point of release. The greatest northward movement was from Cape Canaveral, Florida, in January to South Carolina 168 days later, a distance of 260 miles.

White shrimp are very susceptible to cold water temperatures in the winter. A temperature of less than 47 degrees Fahrenheit is usually lethal to them. Thus, a very cold winter, such as the one in Brunswick County in 1988, leads to a poor harvest in the following summer and fall. In 1988, less than 7,000 pounds of white shrimp were taken, compared with over 290,000 pounds the following year, when the winter temperatures moderated.

The population of white shrimp is not only affected by the weather, but also by shrimpers who drag for them before they have a chance to develop and spread their population out into the ocean. Toward the end of July 1991, for example, the North Carolina Division of Marine Fisheries closed the Shallotte and Calabash rivers, most of the Intracoastal Waterway, and part of the Cape Fear River to shrimp and crab trawlers to protect the small white shrimp.

The known range of white shrimp is from Fire Island, New York, to Cape Canaveral, Florida; in the Gulf of Mexico from Pensacola, Florida, to Campeche, Mexico; off Cuba; and off Jamaica. On the Atlantic coast, they are found on the muddy bottom from the water's edge to seventeen fathoms.

The Shrimping Industry

The first shrimpers in North Carolina may have been Indians of the Cape Fear region. Incomplete historical accounts suggest that Indians caught shrimp with the use of dip nets, seines, and leafy weirs. California, however, was the first state to develop shrimping as a commercial venture. In 1869, eight boats run by Italian fishermen using seines were engaged in shrimping off the California coast. A few years later, Chinese immigrants began shrimping, shipping large quantities of dried shrimp to China. In 1880, some 1,200,000 pounds of shrimp valued at $124,000 were landed in California, more than in any other state. In that year, for example, North Carolina landed only 63,000 pounds of shrimp.[2]

The shrimping industry in North Carolina dates back to the 1880s. Confined to Wilmington and the vicinity, shrimping at

---

[2]Much of the early history of shrimping in North Carolina is drawn from R. E. Earll's "North Carolina and its Fisheries," in *The Fisheries and Fishing Industries of the United States* by G. B. Goode (Washington, D.C.: Government Printing Office, 1884–87), and from an unsigned report entitled "The History of the Shrimping Industry in North Carolina: a Preliminary Report," located in the files of the *Brunswick Beacon*, Shallotte, North Carolina.

that time was an insignificant business. There was practically no market for the shrimp at home, and no one could figure out how to establish a trade with large Northern cities. In 1880, the total landings in the Wilmington area were about five thousand bushels. Nearly half of that amount was sold locally for food, and the other half was used for bait and fertilizer.

Before 1872, most of the shrimp in the Wilmington area were caught with skim nets. That same year, the shrimp seine was introduced. Fitted with weights on the bottom and floats on the top, this new net better enabled fishermen to harvest the

Chaffing gear
(or hula skirt)

bottom-dwelling shrimp. The landings of shrimp began to increase at a rapid rate during the next several years, and by 1915, Brunswick County had replaced New Hanover County as the center of the industry.

The great revolution in shrimping, however, came with the introduction of the otter trawl. Here was a net that enabled shrimpers to extend their fishing area beyond the waters close to shore and out into the ocean. What made this net innovative and suited to deeper waters were the two large boards — called "otter boards" or "doors" — attached to the mouth of the net that caused it to spread open in the water as the boat moved forward. Modified in design over the years and with new arrangements of weights and floats, the otter trawl is essentially the same as the nets used in commercial shrimping to this day. Developed from the beam trawl in England and introduced to the New England fisheries in the 1890s, the otter trawl was first used in shrimping about the turn of the century. By 1917, it was widely used both in the Gulf and along the south Atlantic coast.

According to the *Wilmington Dispatch*, the otter trawl was introduced into North Carolina by a young fisherman from Seabright, New Jersey, named Samuel Thompson. Reporting on the funeral of Samuel Thompson in March of 1916, the newspaper states,

> It was Mr. Thompson who brought the first deep-sea shrimp net to Southport. . . . He taught the Southport fishermen to catch shrimp. Because of this a great industry has sprung up here and during the past two years hundreds of dollars have been placed into circulation. A local shrimp

factory has been built, and several carloads of shrimp have been brought here from Florida waters.... All Southport, and especially those interested in the shrimp industry, owe to him a debt of gratitude . . . and had he lived he would no doubt [have] proven himself to be a leader in the development of the Southport fishing industry.

Another local newspaper reported that by the end of 1916, there were over fifty boats using the new gear. Within ten years, more than four times as many pounds of shrimp were taken with otter trawls than with all the other nets combined. By 1945, nearly 95 percent of all the shrimp caught in North Carolina were taken by otter trawls.

The otter trawl not only opened up the ocean for shrimping, but also necessitated the development of new boats to accommodate the nets. Prior to the introduction of the otter trawl, fishermen usually worked in waters close to the shore in sailboats, rowboats, or other nonpowered vessels. In order to acquire enough power to pull the otter trawls so that the water forced the boards to spread the nets, fishermen required powerboats. The earliest shrimp boats were open skiffs about twenty feet long driven by small gasoline engines. By the early 1920s, the first decked trawlers were in use, the sort built by the Varnam family, whose design is still in use today. This design may have developed from Mediterranean workboats similar to the Greek boats used in the sponge industry off the coast of Florida.

The increase in shrimp landings soon caught the attention of businessmen. In 1915, Richard Dosher and William St. George opened a shrimp factory up the Elizabeth River near Southport. Equipped with modern canning machinery, the Dosher–St. George shrimp factory packed thousands of cans of shrimp daily. That same year, a Mr. F. S. Webster from Scituate, Massachusetts, opened a cannery in Shallotte to process crabs, shrimp, and other seafood from the waters of that area. By 1916, the Dosher–St. George factory employed 150 people. Children apparently comprised a significant portion of the work force, for the *Wilmington Morning Star* of September 23, 1916, reported that the company was experiencing difficulty "in getting all that they wanted, due somewhat to children being at school, many colored children working in the picking rooms."

Refrigeration and the railroads were of great significance in the development of the shrimping industry. They provided the means whereby people in Northern states could purchase fresh shrimp, something they might otherwise only enjoy during their visits to the South. In North Carolina, refrigeration was achieved primarily by icing down fresh shrimp for shipment.

Although the Dosher–St. George cannery made some shipments of fresh, iced shrimp to Northern states, it was primarily devoted to canning shrimp. In 1919, T. H. Lindsey, Charles Hewitt, and W. J. Weeks formed the first company in Southport dedicated to packing and shipping fresh shrimp. Within a year, it shipped thirty refrigerator cars of shrimp to various parts of the United States. At different times during the season, the company also shipped ten- and fifteen-barrel lots to New York, Philadelphia, Baltimore, Chicago, Milwaukee, and other Northern cities.

By the 1930s, the most important market for shrimp outside of the state was New York City. Approximately 98 percent of North Carolina shrimp not consumed locally were sold to wholesalers in New York, especially the Fulton Fish Market, during the next several years. Trucks gradually began to replace refrigerated railway cars as the primary means of transporting the shrimp, enabling shipments to reach the New York market within twenty-four hours.

Shrimping and the fishing industry in general suffered greatly during World War II. Production dropped, the building of new boats decreased, and seven hundred fishing vessels were taken over by the government during the war years. Fuel was rationed, and it was difficult to acquire spare parts for engines and fishing gear. The scarcity of twine and rope made it difficult to buy new nets and repair old ones. There was also a

Top of the net with floats draped over one of the large doors used to spread out the nets in the water

shortage of manpower to run the boats, since thousands of fishermen entered the armed services and the war industries. The threat of German submarines offshore further limited the business of the more than five hundred fishermen who had been working around the Southport area.

The shrimping industry expanded greatly following the war, and by 1952, shrimp had become the most valuable seafood product in the United States. Once viewed as material for fertilizer or bait, shrimp gradually won consumers' acceptance on a grand scale. New marketing techniques, packaging techniques, and products, such as quick-frozen shrimp, and the proliferation of seafood restaurants around the country also furthered interest.

The first recorded shrimp catch in Brunswick County was for the year 1897, when 2,496 pounds of shrimp were caught at a value of $125.[3] One may derive some idea of the desirability and availability of seafood by noting that in that same year, fishermen hauled in 333,100 pounds of mullet worth $9,942, some 24,000 pounds of turtles (most of which were probably loggerheads, now on the endangered-species list) worth $1,920, and 400,000 clams worth $22,500.

By 1918, however, shrimp was becoming an important cash crop in Brunswick County. In that year, 370,000 pounds of

---

[3]The statistics for landings of shrimp and other species were provided by Paul Phalen, statistics coordinator for the North Carolina Division of Marine Fisheries. The data on landings from 1889 to 1967 are from *Synopsis of Marine Fisheries of North Carolina* by A. F. Chestnut and Harry S. Davis (Raleigh: University of North Carolina Sea Grant Program, 1975). The data since 1978 has been collected through a cooperative program between the North Carolina Division of Marine Fisheries and the National Marine Fisheries Service. The historic (pre-1978) data was collected by NMFS.

shrimp were harvested at a value of $11,000. With the beginning of round-bottom shrimp-boat building in the 1920s, the annual catch began to rise. The *Wilmington Morning Star* of February 1, 1920, reported, "Southport is enjoying the best shrimp and mullet season it has ever experienced, according to a statement made yesterday by Captain J. E. Bowen, of the 'Seven Marys,' a launch which has been shrimping off the river bar near Southport. Captain Bowen reported that the larger boats engaged in this industry off Southport this season averaged from 25 to 70 bushels a day, although some of the smaller craft have only obtained about 12 bushels a day."

In 1928, Brunswick County fishermen brought in 587,735 pounds of shrimp valued at $19,630, and in 1934, the catch more than doubled to 1,309,900 pounds valued at $40,547. That number doubled again by 1945 to an astonishing figure of 2,903,300 pounds valued at $232,264, which remains the largest total catch on record. State officials in the Division of Marine Fisheries are unable to explain why there was such a large catch that year. One official in charge of data management told us that "the high landings in 1945 may be an artifact of sampling procedures or a real indication of catch." Our guess is that with shrimping curtailed during World War II, the waters were ripe with shrimp in 1945, and that the demand for them increased along with their price. The average annual catch, however, dropped to between 300,000 and 900,000 pounds during the next forty years. The official landing statistics for Brunswick County since 1983 are included in the appendix on pages 173–74.

These shrimp landings have a peculiar local significance that needs to be put in perspective. Most of the shrimp caught in Brunswick County are sold and eaten locally. When the tourist returns home, the odds are that the shrimp he or she buys from a grocery chain or eats in a restaurant are from another country. According to statistics from the National Marine Fisheries Service, 75 percent of the shrimp eaten in this country are imported. The major exporters of shrimp are China, Ecuador, Mexico, India, and Thailand. These countries have a well-developed system of aquaculture. That is, they raise shrimp in large ponds the year round, rather than dragging for them seasonally as in the United States. Shrimpers in the Gulf and along the south Atlantic coast complain that these imports lower the market price that they are paid, driving some of them out of the business.

Americans' craving for shrimp caused the total supply of domestic and foreign shrimp to rise from 424 million pounds in 1979 to 767 million pounds in 1988. That represents an astonishing 80-percent increase in the amount of shrimp sold in the United States. In 1988, Americans ate 598 million pounds of foreign shrimp, for which wholesalers paid $1.7 billion.

Aquaculture in the United States, which was successfully developed in Alabama, is essentially limited to the production of catfish, crawfish, and trout. Experts believe that labor and energy costs are too high to produce a profitable harvest of shrimp in the relatively short season available in this country. In tropical countries, shrimp farmers can raise two and a half crops each year. The more temperate climate in the United States, however, would allow aquaculturists to raise only one crop. A late freeze, a disease, or reduced oxygen levels in the water could kill the entire year's crop. Needless to say, however, if such a program were put into place, it would almost certainly drive hundreds of ocean shrimpers out of the business.

Net hanging from one of the outriggers

The *Capt. N. C. II* approaching
Bellamy's Fish House to unload its cargo

THE BUG HUNTERS

*T*he shrimp boat is elegant in its simplicity of design. Averaging sixty-five feet in length, the hull typically encloses a three-hundred-horsepower Cummins or Caterpillar diesel engine. Most of the boats in the Holden Beach area have one screw, although there are a few twin-screws as well. On deck, the pilothouse encloses the navigational equipment. Behind the pilothouse lies the galley, containing a stove, sink, toilet, and small bunks. Many boats also have television sets to help the crew pass the time in the evening or other times they are not working.

On the rear deck directly behind the pilothouse are the hydraulic winches that pull in the nets. On either side of the mast are the two outriggers, long steel poles that support the nets. When the boats are in port, the outriggers are raised in an upright position. At sea, they are lowered to hold the two (sometimes four) nets as they are dragged along the bottom of the ocean. At the end of each outrigger is a steel weight resembling an anvil. These weights are the stabilizers that steady the outriggers as they pull the nets across the ocean bottom. Connected to each net are two large wooden "doors" that plane in the water like kites to hold the mouth of the net open to trap the shrimp. Tickler chains are attached to the bottoms of the nets to stir up the white shrimp from the bottom and drive them into the nets.

The nets, made of bonded nylon, range in size from thirty-five to forty-five feet in length. When they are dropped over the sides of the boat, they balloon out under the water as the doors spread them apart. In addition to the two large nets, there is a small one called a "try net," which is also attached to an outrigger. This net is lowered every twenty minutes or so and then retrieved to sample the catch. If the try net contains a sufficient number of shrimp, the captain will continue to work that area of the bottom. If the number of shrimp is too small, or if the net contains too many fish, he will direct the boat to another area and employ the try net again. Frequently, the captain will test the area with the try net before having the big nets dropped over the sides. Once he begins dragging, however, he will continue testing the catch every twenty minutes with the try net to ensure that he is optimizing his use of fuel and time in gathering the shrimp.

Finally, there is the hold in the rear deck, where the culled shrimp are stored. The hold is filled with ice before the boat sets out. When a catch is brought on board, one of the crew pulls a line that opens the bottom of the net, and the contents spill onto the deck. This pile of wriggling and flapping creatures contains not only shrimp, but also various fish, stingrays, an occasional shark, shells, and assorted trash. The crew then separates the shrimp from this tangle of wildlife and shovels them into the ice in the hold. They throw the fish, rays, shells, and other creatures back into the sea. They may keep a few edible fish for themselves, but most are returned to the ocean. The hundreds of sea gulls that follow these boats, however, manage to enjoy a frenzied feast in their wake.

Anyone who has simply wrestled with a tangled fishing line must marvel at the smooth deployment of the large nets through an elaborate array of pulleys and ropes that dominates the rear deck. What appears to be a chaos of mesh, ropes, floats, and chains becomes, under the experienced hands of these fishermen, an artful cast to the bottom of the ocean.

The captain of a shrimp boat is a hunter, a navigator, armed with fish scopes, depth finders, radar, and, most importantly, experience, who searches the ocean bottom in the hope of netting a creature about the size of his thumb. Unlike the macho sportfisherman out to catch a record-sized marlin, blue, or shark that he can display on his office wall, the captain of a shrimper is content to pull in a netful of creatures each weighing less than an ounce, which will be devoured by some stranger in a local restaurant. Area residents acknowledge this irony by calling shrimps "bugs" and shrimpers "bug hunters." One of the local shrimp boats, in fact, is called the *Bug Hunter*.

The captain of a shrimp boat, especially if he owns his own rig, is a proud and tough-minded individual who, after years of experience as a deck hand on others' boats, has finally achieved the American dream of self-reliance. The shrimper's relationship with his boat is not unlike that of the cowboy with his horse. The shrimper has the privilege of naming his boat, the responsibility of feeding it and caring for it, and the joy of riding it across the plains of water on one adventure after another. His boat gives him a temporary freedom from "the hill," as the watermen call the land, and affords him a priceless independence as he gathers and brings home his bounty from the sea.

Seated in his pilothouse behind the wheel, steering his boat slowly through the morning mist towards deep water miles away from land, he feels himself to be in control of his destiny, at least for the next few hours or days. With ample food aboard, plenty of fuel in the tanks, the nets draped at the ready from the tall outriggers, and the hold full of ice awaiting the first catch, the captain and his crew of two men may share a thermos of coffee as the boat, guided by Loran C, moves towards an area of the ocean that may, the captain suspects from past experience, yield a rich harvest of white shrimp. Surrounded by the accustomed sounds of the waves splashing hard against the burly boat, the deep rumble of the diesel engine felt in the feet and legs, and the occasional squawk of the marine CB radio, the captain steers away from underwater obstacles known to hang the nets, checks his fish scope, and alerts his crew to ready the nets.

The outriggers are lowered, and the nets and heavy wooden doors are pushed overboard. Within seconds after hitting the water and ballooning out, the huge nets create so much friction that they jerk the boat to a slow crawl. The great torque of the diesel engine, however, allows the boat to continue forward despite the enormous drag. The boat is now moving not unlike a plane or an automobile pulling a huge parachute behind it. Fuel is being consumed at a dizzying rate, and unless shrimp are entering the nets, the boat will have to move on to other waters. The captain therefore lowers the try net to sample the catch. It comes up with a good number of white shrimp and only a few trash fish. The fish scope confirms that this is a workable area, and the captain steers the boat around to continue dragging the hot spot. It looks like a good day.

In order to retrieve the catch, the hydraulic winches pull the entire nets close to the boat, the doors riding up above the gunnels. At that point, one of the deck hands throws out a "lazy line," a cable with a hook that fastens around the portion of the net containing the catch. It is called a lazy line because it enables the shrimper to land the catch without having to pull the entire net onto the boat. Since the nets are now riding high in the water, the catch must be retrieved quickly to avoid damage from the turbulence of the boat's wake. First the bottom of one net and then the other is hauled in with the winch and suspended above the rear deck. The bags are then opened, and thousands of glistening shrimp, along with hundreds of fish and shells and odd pieces of trash, fall squirming and flapping in a shower onto the deck. As the crew culls the shrimp from the rest of the catch and throws the fish and trash back into the sea, the captain steers his boat to another area he hopes will fill his nets.

The captain's worst fear is that his nets will get caught on an underwater obstruction. Despite his charts of all known obstructions and his ability to navigate around them, the inevitable sometimes happens, and he must maneuver his boat back and forth and around in hopes of pulling the nets free. A minor tear may be repaired at sea, but if a net is seriously torn by an obstruction or by a captured shark, then he must return to the hill and lose precious fishing time.

After two or three days of fishing, the captain brings his boat to a local fish house. One of his crew goes down into the hold and shovels the shrimp off the chopped ice into large buckets that are hoisted on pulleys onto the dock. After the shrimp are unloaded, they are dumped on large wooden tables in the fish house. Standing by to dehead the shrimp are about a dozen people, mostly women and young boys, relatives and friends of the fishermen previously alerted to the incoming boat. After the shrimp are deheaded, they are weighed, and the captain is paid for his catch by the tail weight.

While the captain is working at sea, he is his own man, a hunter tracking down the elusive prey. The sense of freedom he enjoys in his water world, however, is tempered by his recognition of growing economic and environmental problems that constrain and threaten his independence. The captains we interviewed all expressed a profound anxiety about the future of their livelihood. Unlike the shrimpers of the preceding decades, under whose tutelage they learned their craft, these men are facing difficulties their parents and grandparents never dreamed of.

The *Capt. N. C. II*

William Varnam is the captain of the *Capt. N. C. II*, a boat built and owned by Norman Bellamy. A short, thin man in his early thirties, William has been shrimping since 1976, having started out as a deck hand. Like most of the Varnams in the area, he knows he is related somehow to just about every other Varnam (or Varnum) in Supply and Varnamtown, but he is not sure exactly how. He dreams of one day owning his own shrimp boat but in the meantime seems quite happy to be in charge of the *Capt. N. C. II*.

We first met William in September of 1990 at Bellamy's Fish House, located on the Intracoastal

William Varnam, captain of the *Capt. N. C. II*

Waterway overlooking the south bank of Holden Beach, where he was unloading a catch of shrimp he had brought in the night before.

There was another shrimp boat at the dock, and the *Capt. N. C. II* was tied up on the far side of that boat. It was nine o'clock in the morning, and a call had gone out to several of the women in the area informing them to come to work, that the *Capt. N. C. II* was getting ready to unload. William's wife dropped him off at the dock in her car a few minutes after nine. Wearing blue jeans, a clean white T-shirt, tall green rubber boots, and a baseball-type cap (a ubiquitous headpiece in the area), William headed to his boat to bring it alongside the dock while the other boat moved away. He switched on the ignition, bringing the diesel engine to life, put the propeller in reverse, and backed the boat into the Waterway while the other boat cleared the dock. He maneuvered the large vessel with a practiced agility, as if he were parallel parking an automobile.

Norman Bellamy's son-in-law, Wycuff Skipper, took charge of the dockside operation, getting the hoist and empty buckets ready. The women began arriving. They gathered inside the fish house around the large wooden table where the shrimp would be piled and deheaded. A young man about eighteen years old named Burton Smith, who works as a deck hand on the *Capt. N. C. II*, jumped into the hold of the boat wearing tall rubber boots and a work-worn cap and began shoveling the shrimp into a bucket lowered down to him. When the bucket was filled, it was hoisted onto the dock and then carried into the fish house, where it was dumped onto the long deheading table.

While this operation was under way, William sat on the

boat's railing and spoke to us about shrimping. Mr. Bellamy, he explained, wants to retire and sell the *Capt. N. C. II* and his fish house, and he hopes one day to be able to buy the boat. This is not a step that William takes lightly. He is keenly aware of the problems that shrimp-boat captain-owners face.

"There's all this business about turtle-excluder nets," he began, then turned quickly to the situation in the Middle East. "There's the crisis in the Gulf, and the price of fuel is going up. No more shrimp than there are out there, that's going to hurt. The price of shrimp is falling every week.

Shrimp is lifted out of the hold onto the dock by an electric pulley. Ed Robinson (*rear*) works the pulley as Wycuff Skipper, who manages the fish house, guides the basket onto the dock.

"The good-sized shrimp right here," he continued, pointing to his catch being unloaded, "four or five years ago would bring somewhere in the neighborhood of $5.00 a pound. Right now, they're $3.15. Last week, they were $3.37 cleared to the boat. Fuel going up, price of shrimp going down. On your summer shrimping, you can get a fairly good price out of them with the tourists around, but they're smaller shrimp. But after they leave, you end up having to put your shrimp on a truck, and he carries them to the breaders. The breaders' price for shrimp is lower than what you get out of them locally."

Under siege not only from skyrocketing fuel prices, increased insurance rates, new state and federal regulations, and too many shrimpers for the supply of shrimp, William was noticeably disturbed by the rapid rise of recreational fishing that threatens an already diminished supply of shrimp. "Fishermen tried to get the Cape Fear River closed to fishing until the shrimp got to a certain size," he said. "There are a lot of shrimp up there. We don't knock them for trying to make a living up there, but they're hurting themselves as well as us by catching shrimp before they've grown. If the state had closed the river and let the shrimp grow, there'd be enough for everybody. The recreational fishermen pull smaller net webbing than we do, so they're catching everything there is on the bottom. We're pulling an inch and three-quarters stretch mesh while they're pulling an inch and a half. They're catching everything."

The following year, the state did, indeed, close part of the Cape Fear River and other waterways to dragging while the shrimp were growing to marketable size and moving out into the ocean. William's complaint about the dual standards for the size of the nets' mesh, however, raises an issue that continues to plague the commercial shrimper. The difference between the inch and three-quarters mandated by law for the shrimper and the inch and a half allowed the recreational fisherman may seem to be negligible. The slightly smaller mesh in the recreational fisherman's nets, however, enables him to trap thousands of juvenile shrimp before they have a chance to mature and enter the nets of the commercial shrimper. The different standards for net sizes may have made sense when sportfishing was a limited, sporadic activity, but in recent years, with the rapid development of tourism in the area, it has become a major business.

As visitors who have spent many summer weeks poking blindly into the sand under four feet of water in hopes of plucking up a sand dollar or an interesting-looking shell, we were very curious about what treasures a shrimper, dragging huge nets across the bottom of the ocean miles from shore, might dredge up from the mysterious depths. William seemed pleased to disclose some of the secrets of the deep: "On an easterly wind, the fish come into the beach. They get bad at times. We'd see them piled up deep on the deck. Deck loads of fish. We sort the shrimp out of the fish and push the fish back overboard, and the birds go for the fish.

"When you see them birds flocking after them fish, there's great big old sharks down there. Yeah, mingling in with them fish. Big old sharks. We get sharks in our nets all the time. They'll cut your nets. We caught one last year that had his mouth into the webbing, and we were pulling our nets along the side, and as we were picking the bags up he ripped the whole net in two. We had to quit. He swum away after he tore the nets in two. He was just hunting a way out, that's all. It took two days to sew that net up."

Fishermen were getting paid eighty cents a pound for shark that year, but a shrimp net is obviously not an economical way to haul one in. William said that he had heard the Japanese are fond of shark fins in a stew. "You have to soak shark meat for a while—it's like venison—to get the wild flavor out. It's pretty, white meat, and it don't have bones in it. I've never tried it on the grill. I've fried it before, but I imagine it would be pretty good on the grill."

William went on to list some of the other surprises he has found in his nets, beginning with something he discovered after Hurricane Hugo: "After the storm down there at Holden Beach, we caught a drain tile. How it got out there, I'll never know. I've caught a vacuum cleaner, gas grill, tin, steps off some of the beach houses, electrical wire, fence wire, the sort they run along the beach to hold the sand—it'll tie your nets together—tree stumps, cinder blocks, and tires. On this boat here, I caught a flagpole in the net. You catch all kinds of stuff: manta rays, stingrays, some about as big as your deck. Some of them will pull your boat right on around. I have known them to tear your nets in two."

The tons of wreckage that Hurricane Hugo carried from the land to the bottom of the sea caused shrimpers endless headaches. As William explained, "The hurricane run all the shrimp out of the creeks because of the high tides. Shrimp were scattered everywhere. You could drag most anywhere to catch some shrimp. Of course, you had to put up with all the junk that got swung off these beach houses. A lot of boats tore up their nets right and left. One net will cost in the neighborhood of $1,200."

Once a shrimper is out on the ocean dragging his nets, he has a fair amount of spare time to relax. Some boats have television sets or radios to help while the time away. "Things are slack out there right now," William declared. "We average our nets on the bottom about two hours before we wind them up. That will keep two crew members busy for about thirty to forty minutes. Plenty of time to sit around. We probably average working about two to three hours a day, as far as picking up shrimp goes. A lot of time, when the fish is bad, we're pushing fish off the deck all day long."

Noticing some onions hanging off the pilothouse in a net bag, we asked him who does the cooking. "Anybody who gets around the stove," he replied. "First come, first served. Whoever gets the hungriest first gets back there and starts cooking." He then told a story about one of his crew members. "I heard one of them say that we're out of groceries, that we've been out here two or three days and ain't finding that much, and we're going to head for the dock. I tell him, 'Son, you ain't never out of groceries when you're out here on the boat. There's plenty of fish and shrimp on the boat. As long as you got a gallon of cooking oil and a bag of flour, you won't go hungry.'"

We met William again in March of the next year. He was inspecting the bottom of the *Capt. N. C. II*, which was in dry dock at the end of Old Ferry Road. Hauled out of the water on a rail carriage by hydraulic winches, the boat looked enormous. It was the first time we had ever seen a keel cooler, snaking tubes of copper pipes beneath the keel's waterline that carry water to cool the engine. The five-finned propeller, about five feet in diameter, seemed hardly large enough to drive the heavy boat and pull the huge nets through the water. The boat's bottom was to be scraped and cleaned with power hoses, and the entire boat was to be repainted. The *Capt. N. C. II* had suffered the onslaught of salt water and rough weather and was ready for renovation.

Another crew member of the *Capt. N. C. II* we talked with in September was Ed Robinson, a man in his early sixties. Ed specializes in net making and repairing. A Louisianan, he retired to the Holden Beach area after he retired from the navy in 1978. His wife's family is from the area. "I learned net making from Norman Bellamy," he said. "Of course, I had the basic knowledge of knots and cables and all that already."

Keenly aware that the art of net making and repairing is, like shrimping itself, gradually disappearing, Ed hopes to pass on his craft by teaching a net-making class at Brunswick Community College in nearby Supply. "There's a lot of art to net making," he said. "If people don't wind up learning it, it's going to be a lost art. If someone has a net they want to repair, or if they want to build one, they come to class. You have to have a good, sharp knife and a net needle and a good, strong pair of hands, and that's it."

Standing in Bellamy's Fish House surrounded by piles of green shrimp nets, Ed gave us a brief introduction to nets and net making: "The webbing comes in sheets—two hundred squares across the sheet and however long you need it. They rig them in different ways. They have a three-tongued net, a mongoose net, four-seam, two-seam, flat nets, balloon nets, and semiballoon nets. It's just according to what the people on a boat want. They determine that by where they're fishing. One net will work better in the mud, for example, than it will in the sand." He picked up a net from the floor. "This is what will work here. It's a four-seam balloon with a mongoose under a tongue in it, with doors on each side and a center cable coming in to hold that tongue up. It's like a bib. They'll put floats on it.

"Every so often, you have to dip them. That's what that green stuff is. The netting we buy comes white, no color at all. We soak the netting in net dip, and it protects it, keeps it from rotting. The dip has a lacquer base to it, almost like paint. If you didn't put that on them, you could drag for a week and there wouldn't be any bottom on them. You put the nets in a big vat, push them under the dip, and they soak that dip up, and then you take them out to drain. Once they drain, you stretch them out to dry so that they don't get all into one wad. If they do, you got a problem."

Most of the shrimp nets include a "chaffing gear," a colorful web of nylon netting resembling the tail on a kite, which protects the nets from wearing out as they drag along the ocean bottom. A Texas rig, however, uses a tickler chain, a short length of heavy chain that digs into the ocean bottom to stir up the shrimp.

Although Ed works mostly with shrimp nets, he has custom-designed nets for specialized fishing. The size of the net's mesh and the material it is made from depend upon the fisherman's catch. "Out in the ocean," Ed explained, "a seine net must use two-and-a-half-inch mesh. That's something that was enacted into law this year. In the spring, the spots in the Waterway require a smaller net."

He is especially proud of a net he built for a shark fisherman: "I built a net 250 yards long out of eight-inch stretch for a fellow who wanted it for shark fishing. It was heavy net. We had to dip it the same way we do our shrimp nets. Those sharks can tear a net up, but the monofilament doesn't tear as bad as the shrimp nets. This fellow—his name's Freddie McGinn, a big fellow, around three hundred pounds—lives out of Little River down here. That's all he does for a living—shark fishing. He ships them to places like New York. They've just enacted legislation whereby recreational fishermen can only catch two sharks a day and commercial fishermen only so many pounds a trip. They ship the shark fins over to the Orient, where they think it has some mystical powers."

A fish house cat in shrimp heaven

William Varnam (*left*) and Burton Smith (*right*)
examine the weathered hull of the *Capt. N. C. II*

After talking with us, Ed joined in at the deheading table,
where several women were busily at work. After the buckets of
shrimp were dumped in the middle of the long table, the women,
each using an old license plate, scraped a small pile of shrimp
in front of them. Working with both hands at a remarkable
pace, they pinched off the shrimp heads between their thumbs
and forefingers, occasionally stopping to shovel the heads into
a trash pile and to scrape up another batch of shrimp. Although
none of the women was wearing gloves, there is always the
danger of getting one's finger pricked in the deheading process.
The tough carapace that covers the head of a shrimp comes to
a sharp, barbed point that can easily pierce the flesh of a
deheader's hand, causing it to swell and even turn yellow. A

young woman working in a Holden Beach grocery store told us that she worked one summer deheading shrimp but had to quit after she got stuck. Her hand swelled up, turned yellow, and became too painful to allow her to continue in her job.

The women who worked around the deheading table were very silent. They all knew each other, and they had been doing this work for years. Occasionally, they exchanged a few remarks about local goings-on. Perhaps our presence inhibited them. We asked one of them what they do with the heads, and she said they throw them into the Waterway for the crabs. No one seemed to pay any attention to the two cats that lived in the fish house. As the shrimp were dumped on the table, the cats would jump up, each grab a shrimp, and dive beneath the table to eat it. They did this five or six times before they had their fill and disappeared.

The *Andrea Dawn*

The first shrimp boat we saw up close was in 1983, when we went to Capt'n Pete's Seafood House to buy some fish. Docked alongside the fish house was the *Amor*, an eighty-foot trawler owned by Pete Singletary, known as Capt'n Pete. A shrimper turned entrepreneur, Pete had the boat built for him by Weston Varnam in 1978, fished with it for several years, and sold it to Danny Galloway in 1989. Danny renamed it the *Andrea Dawn*.

We met Danny in September 1990 when he was refueling his boat after unloading a catch of shrimp at Capt'n Pete's dock. A small, stocky man in his forties, Danny was wearing a faded maroon cap that he later informed us he had dredged out of the ocean in one of his nets. Given the recent increase in the cost of diesel fuel, Danny did not look too happy as he was pumping gallons of kerosene into his fuel tanks. "The *Andrea Dawn* holds about 6,000 gallons," he said. "I never fill her up, just put that stick in her to see how low I am. Right now, I have a half a tank. You use about 150 gallons every twelve hours, about 300 gallons every clock."

The *Andrea Dawn*, (formerly *Amor*), built by Weston Varnam and owned and captained by Danny Galloway, docked at Capt'n Pete's Seafood House

Standing on the deck of the boat near Danny was a young man named Greg Holden, who works as a deck hand. Greg is a distant relative of the Holden family that developed the island. Neatly dressed and well spoken, Greg seemed more like a college undergraduate than a shrimper. "He's a treasure hunter," quipped Galloway. We told them that the tourists who see a shrimp boat out on the ocean often wonder what is going on in the boat. Danny answered, "We're on the boat wondering what's going on on the land."

Danny was most eager to talk about the problems created for shrimpers by the mandated turtle-excluder devices (TEDs) and by the degradation of the environment. The previous year, he had been forced to pull the turtle excluder every hour and a half, releasing any turtles that may have gotten caught in his nets so that they could avoid drowning. After the first of September, this restriction had been removed, but the loss of shrimp caused by the turtle-excluder device — many shrimp get

Danny Galloway in the stern of the *Andrea Dawn*

released from the nets along with the turtles — still rankled him.

"The boat don't kill that many to start with," he said. "We're just taking the rap. There's somebody up yonder sitting there figuring out something for somebody else to do. Now, we kill a turtle or two, but nothing like you read about in the papers. If a turtle comes up on the beach when a shrimp boat's working in the area, whether the boat's killed him or not — the turtle might have died of old age or might have gotten caught in a gill net or got hit by a boat prop — they say a shrimp boat's killed him. The further you get south, the worse your turtle problem is. I've talked to fellows who have been down there, and there are places you can catch a lot of turtles. But up here, we don't catch all that many."

It may well be that Danny was correct in thinking that more turtles are trapped in the nets of shrimpers south of Brunswick County, but there is no question that even the trawlers off the North Carolina coast have killed a fair share. Several Texas shrimpers recently interviewed on television also protested that they have seldom caught any turtles in their nets. One fisherman summed up the frustration of all shrimpers when he said that if he had a hole in his net as big as the one mandated by the TED, he would immediately pull in his nets and repair them. Here is the classic conflict between already hard-strapped small businesses and those who would protect an endangered species. Many of the shrimpers in Brunswick County are developing a siege mentality as they see their profits continue to dwindle under the pressure of foreign competition, an increasing number of shrimpers, and new federal and state regulations.

"The price of shrimp doesn't go up," Danny complained. "There are too many imports. It used to be around here if we had a bad year, the price of shrimp would go up. But now it's not like that. A man can just pick up his phone and have a truckload brought in at what the market price is. So whether we have a bad year or a good year doesn't determine the price of shrimp. And interest rates and insurance are way up. Fuel is way up."

Danny's biggest complaint, however, was about the degradation of the environment: "There's just too much pressure put on the environment. Nature and people don't go together, really. This river used to support this whole neighborhood. When you get upriver, people are oystering, clamming, fishing, and farming—to make a living. When you put condos beside the water, you put millions of gallons of sewerage into it. The first thing that happens, the oysters are polluted, the clams are polluted. Everybody staying in the condos wants to go out on the river. If he does nothing but turn over shells, he's killing something or other that something feeds on. And when you get thousands of people stalking one place, you end up with a problem. That's what's happening to the shrimp, really. You get too many boats running down the river. Everybody's got a boat. If he's got nothing else, he's got a cast net he wants to tug.

"Our main shrimp comes from Cape Fear, the biggest river. They got paper plants, steel plants all the way up the middle of the city. While they're trying to clean it up now, for years they dumped raw sewerage into the river. That will do away with us quicker than the marketing. There are enough local sales here that you'd probably get by with. Sometimes, we get a little bit better than market price. I'm afraid there's just not going to be any more shrimp."

Like William Varnam, Danny complained about the fishermen who drag the river before the shrimp have a chance to mature. "The boats that worked in the river got about sixty boxes in a week — probably sixty-pound shrimp," he said. Sixty-pound or sixty-catch shrimp come sixty to the pound. "If they were allowed to grow another five weeks, we could have gotten a hundred boxes of twenty- or thirty-catch shrimp by then, and worth over twice as much money."

Danny then showed us some of the equipment in his wheelhouse. The plotter, which is connected to the Loran,

Inside the pilot house of the *Andrea Dawn* fully equipped with electronic gear

showed by a series of straight and zigzag lines the path the *Andrea Dawn* had followed on its recent trip. The plotter not only records everywhere the boat goes, but it marks with Xs all of the places where Danny or another fisherman has lost a net. Some of the Xs pinpoint the location of rocks that would endanger the boat.

After viewing the recorded path of the *Andrea Dawn*, we were surprised to discover that a shrimp boat does not have the whole sea open to its operation. In fact, it has to work within a narrow range of the water clearly laid out by the plotter. Danny explained, "People see boats dragging, and they think they are dragging the whole ocean. But that's not the way it is. Every inch on that plotter represents seven-tenths of a mile. The whole area we can drag is right there where you can see the marks — about seven miles by ten miles. It's very limited. You can drag all the way down the beach, but you can't drag but a quarter in because of the sand. From half a mile out is rock. So we ain't dragging but three-eighths of a mile up and down the beach. That's why we really don't do as much damage as we get credit for. We're limited to where we can drag, but the fish and the turtles, they're everywhere."

The Loran (*Lo*ng *ra*nge *n*avigation), which receives pulsed radio signals sent out from two different points, enables the captain to know his exact location on the ocean. Danny uses Loran C, a model that has been available over ten years, but he noted that the government has come up with a new navigational system that works off a satellite.

The fish scope, resembling a small, round-screen television, helps to locate fish, mud, rocks, and sand. "It marks the bottom red," Danny explained. "The deeper red, the harder the bottom. That red might turn orange or yellow for mud. If you get a small amount of fish, it'll mark them blue. If you get a large amount of fish, it'll mark them red." He was quick to point out, however, that a fish scope is no substitute for experience. "A certain kind of fish might swim close together, and it'll mark them red. The scope doesn't show you if there are spots or croakers. It's something you got to learn to interpret. It's not foolproof, just an aid."

Next to his fish scope was a bottom recorder, which makes a printout of the contours of the ocean bottom to about six hundred feet. Like all of the electronics in the wheelhouse, this is simply another device to improve the vision and positioning of the bug hunter in his search for the elusive, bottom-feeding prey hidden by tons of dark water.

Although the electronics are helpful aids, Danny knows from his twenty years of experience that "there are certain areas you just learn to drag. To find out if there are any shrimp or not, you usually use the try net. It determines what we do. It tells how long we can tug. If you get a bunch of fish, you can't drag for long. It determines how long we tug and where we tug. If we get a good try, we just turn around and pull that area. Then we just go on looking."

Despite his dedication to shrimping, Danny is keenly aware that he may do more looking than catching in the future. "In South Carolina," he explained, "they stopped night fishing. You can't drag nets at night. It should be like that up here. North Carolina laws are very lax. The bottom's been dragged to death. Nobody knows when to quit. Somebody's dragging it all the time. If you were looking at the past ten to fifteen years, you would see that shrimping is declining. Even the good years now would be less than the good years ten years ago. I don't think the shrimp business will be here in twenty years." Indeed, the statistics for shrimp landings supplied by the North Carolina Division of Marine Fisheries give some support to Danny's pessimism.

The *Capt. N. C.*

We first met Henderson Caison on a rainy September afternoon in 1991. He and his brother Charlie were sitting on the shrimp table in Fulford's Fish House waiting for the rain to stop so that they could work on their boats. Henderson, known as "Hen" to his friends, is a soft-spoken man in his late forties. He has been shrimping for over thirty years and has been the owner-captain of the *Capt. N. C.* since 1975. He knows the waters between Pamlico Sound and Key West as well as anyone, and he is passing on his skills as a shrimper to his son, Henderson, who has been a member of his father's crew for several years now.

Henderson Caison in the pilot house of his boat, the *Capt. N. C.*

Henderson was born just outside of Shallotte and has been drawn to the life of a waterman ever since he was a child. He quit school in his early teens to work on a dredge boat and then met up with a Captain Rudy, who introduced him to shrimping. "I started fishing with an old merchant-marine captain," he said. "He was an unlimited-licensed captain. He could fish anywhere in the world. But he retired from that and got a little old boat, and I went shrimping with him on that. I was only sixteen years old. And I've been shrimping ever since."

Henderson's first shrimp boat was the *Miss Caison*. His brother Wilbur and Norman Bellamy built it for him and Charlie, who shared the ownership and running of the boat. "Every time Norman saw me and my brother Charlie come in with a good catch," he explained, "Norman would say, 'I believe I'll build me another.' I just got tired of hearing him say that, so I said, 'Norman, if you build a boat the way I want, I'll leave the *Miss Caison* and shrimp the new boat for you.'"

The *Capt. N. C.*, docked outside Fulford's Fish House

Henderson recalled that Norman had built a twin-engine party boat, the *Royal Princess*, for a golf company. He asked Norman to build him one like that, with twin engines in it. "So, sure enough," he continued, "Norman went and built one, the *Capt. N. C.* So my brother got him a crew on the *Miss Caison*, and I sold him my half of it. I've owned the *Capt. N. C.* for eighteen years now, and I'm the only captain who's ever been on it. The 'N. C.' stands for Norman Curtis. I carried Norman outside on it. It was the first time Norman was outside on one of his boats." Among Holden Beach shrimpers, going "outside" means going out onto the ocean.

Henderson is proud of his boat and its unusual construction. He emphasized the importance of regular maintenance, and the boat, despite its age, showed that he has given it great care. In fact, the next day, he had it pulled up at Hewitt's Railway to scrub the bottom and paint it.

Charlie Caison grinning out the window of his boat, the *Miss Caison*

He explained some of the features of the *Capt. N. C.*: "My boat has three keels. Two run about halfway up the boat, and the center keel runs nearly up to the stern. When I put it up on the rails, it doesn't need any chocks. If you were to run it up on the hill, it will sit up straight.

"There are two Caterpillar engines in my

boat. I'm not a fanatic about engines. I told Norman that I didn't care how much power I had as long as I had two V-8 engines in it. He's a Caterpillar man. You take a GM—you have to have a left-handed GM engine and a right-handed GM engine for twin screws. With a Caterpillar, you have one engine in forward gear and one in reverse gear and have a left-handed wheel and a right-handed wheel. I have as much power in reverse as I have in forward."

Henderson invited us into the pilothouse of the *Capt. N. C.* The walls were lined with mahogany paneling, as were the walls of the bedrooms. "That's my bedroom there," he pointed out. "It looks as if a bunch of rats have been in there." The interior was much more spacious than one might have judged from the outside. Nearly two decades of constant use gave the atmosphere a thoroughly lived-in appearance. These quarters, after all, were where Henderson had lived for most of the past eighteen years. He was comfortable and relaxed here. It took awhile to sink in, but we came to realize that we had been invited not into a pilothouse but into a home.

Beginning with the plotter, he turned on all his electronic instruments to demonstrate how they operate. "Those dots are hangs, and the lines show where I've been dragging," he explained. "That device has more sense than I've got." He pointed to one dot and said, "That's a hang up the Little River where a boat burned and sunk about three years ago." He then showed us a book containing readings for all the hangs and reefs between Holden Beach and Key West. Several well-thumbed pages of penciled numbers indicated one of the complexities involved in navigating a shrimp boat down the coast.

Then he pointed to a hang near Holden Beach where Billy Caison had recently caught his nets. "That hang is inshore from another bad hang, but there's enough room so that I can drag between them," he said. "Before we had the electronics, we used a certain color house on the hill to line up with to help us get through these hangs. The big water tank and the lighthouse at Southport—when you got to the west of that, you were subject to get this hang. We also used to line ourselves up with the Yaupon pier and a specific house, but Hurricane Hazel took down the pier."

As he turned on the radar to see if there was any rain in the area, he remarked, "I depend on this mess too much. I shouldn't really depend on it. If it goes out, I'm lost." The radar picked up some light rain coming in from the west. He demonstrated the depth recorder next, which showed there to be six feet of water under the boat. Finally, he turned on the fish finder. "If a fish goes underneath me," he explained, "the finder will holler. I had it set one night when we were at anchor. It kept going off with a loud chirping sound, and my son heard it. He looked around and we were still in the same place. Then I jumped up and found that there were fish going underneath us."

The fish finder not only helps to locate fish but can also go off if it detects the bottom of the water. Henderson recalled one night when he wishes he had set the finder: "I had anchored offshore, and while I was sleeping, I heard a noise. I got up and looked around. If I had gone out of the starboard door, I would have seen the strand, but I went out the other door and went back and lay down. By the time I lay down, I felt the boat move again. She drifted and hit the shore, and I ran to fire up them engines, shoved it in gear, and took her off the sand. If I had set the finder, it would have gone off. I was lucky. There was no damage. The only damage it caused was that I couldn't sleep here for about three weeks. Now, I sleep so light it doesn't really do much good."

Earlier in our conversation, Henderson had remarked that a couple of days ago he had been out shrimping in a rather high sea, and that he did not enjoy sleeping when the waves were rolling his boat. We now understood the source of his anxiety. Instead of being rocked to sleep by the swell of the waves, he imagines his boat — his home on the water and his livelihood — slowly drifting into the rocks that lie submerged about a mile and a half off Holden Beach.

Like most fishermen in the area, Henderson shrimps off the Carolinas from the end of May through October. Then he works his way down the coast to St. Augustine. He stays there for three weeks, returns to his family for a week, and then heads back to Florida for another three weeks. "No matter what kind of weather, what color shrimp," he said, "when three weeks is up, I come home. You've got to have a system when you go down there, because it takes so much money to travel back and forth."

He maintains a regular cycle until February, when he returns home for good. He does no shrimping during March, April, and May, using that time to be with his family and to work on his boat. Then, towards the end of May, he begins the work cycle all over again. With the exception of three months during the spring each year, he spends the greater portion of his life within an area of a few square feet. His quarters are spartan, containing only the bare essentials for living and carrying on his work. Paradoxically, he can enjoy a sense of enormous freedom while riding the open sea and its seemingly endless horizon.

The biggest catch Henderson ever brought in was at Key West. He had a twenty-basket drag, amounting to eight hundred pounds. But the most money he ever made in two hours of work was off Georgetown, South Carolina. "That was many years ago," he said ruefully. "In shrimping," he went on, "you go out this week and you might make $1,000 or $1,500. Next week, you might not make $25. You have to have brains enough to figure your money up, estimate your money." Some of the strikers who worked for him, he noted, were unable to budget their money and quit during the weeks that their pay dropped off.

A shrimp boat is not a very secure place. Henderson has had his boat broken into several times — at St. Augustine, Key West, and Georgetown. It has been broken into only once at Holden Beach, but he did not have the boat locked up at the time and did not lose anything valuable. In St. Augustine, his striker stole $700 worth of wrenches from the boat and, as Henderson later discovered, sold them for $50.

More troublesome than the break-ins, however, was a recent event off Georgetown that cost Henderson his shrimp nets. While he and his brother Charlie were shrimping, two Coast Guard boats came out to board his and his brother's boats. Here is Henderson's account of the moment: "One party came to my brother's boat and one to mine. Evidently, the party that came on my boat wanted to make a big show. They tried to say my 'shooter' was wrong. In fact, they didn't know what was wrong. They even called the other cutter and sent another man over here. He got down and measured my turtle shooters and looked up at them and said, 'There's nothing wrong with this man's rig.' He didn't call it 'nets,' he called it 'rig.' But the other man was in charge on my boat, and he had the final word. The man who came over to my boat had just left my brother's boat, and he passed all his nets, and his nets are just like mine.

"All the time this was going on, my nets were hung up. I stayed on that for about six hours, trying to get them off the hang. It was getting dark. And I was as nice to this man as I would be to my mother. I didn't raise my voice. It was getting dark, and the water was rough. I told him it would be dangerous for us to continue trying to get off the hang once it got dark in this rough water. He told me to go ahead and get off the hang.

"I finally got them to get off the stern and go to the bow. Then a line broke, and it struck my striker in the mouth. That made me mad. One of them jumped up and said, 'I'm a paramedic,' and he went back and checked my striker. He said he was all right, that he might need a stitch in his lip. In the meantime, my nets got torn to pieces.

"I've never been harassed like that before in my life. I had always been treated decently. I had to spend more than $3,500 for new nets."

The Coast Guard insisted that the TED was improperly installed and confiscated his torn nets. When he returned home, Henderson contacted his congressmen, and they directed him to two lawyers, one in Washington and one in Wilmington, to handle his case against the Coast Guard. After over four months, he heard from the Washington lawyer that all charges had been dropped and that his nets had been released.

"But I can't go hunt my nets on a rabbit's foot," he protested. "I don't know where they're at. The lawyer didn't tell me where they're at. I've heard nothing from the Coast Guard, nothing from the Marine Fisheries. All I've heard is from the lawyer in Washington. I've heard nothing from the lawyer in Wilmington. They've had my nets since the twenty-second of May. What makes it so bad is that I wasn't guilty. I was in the right. The lawyer said that the Coast Guard was going to bring me my nets. I haven't seen the nets yet. I had to buy a whole new set of nets. What matters worse, I had to push the whole last drag of shrimp overboard."

When we talked with Henderson again in March of 1992, he seemed sadly resigned to the fact that he still had not heard a word about his confiscated nets and probably never would. Independent and proud, he went about the business of repairing a rotten section of his boat's pilothouse in order to ready the *Capt. N. C.* for another vigorous season of shrimping.

Despite such outrageous hardships, Henderson displayed a buoyant spirit as he conjured up memories of his son's recent marriage on the *Capt. N. C.* as it moved down the Intracoastal Waterway. Norman Bellamy, who built the boat and is a preacher, performed the ceremony. Henderson recalled the event with a smile: "I missed the ceremony because I was steering the boat. I didn't run the boat fast, I just idled it, and everyone said they hardly knew the boat was moving. Everything went smoothly. There was a little sailboat that came up behind us. He wouldn't pass me. I believe he knew what was going on. He just stayed behind me the whole time. Everybody was dressed up on the stern. He must have figured out that something unusual was going on."

The North Carolina shrimpers are a conservative, tightly knit family of sorts. Henderson's comment upon his son's marriage reflected this strong sense of regionalism: "My son's wife is a nurse, well educated. She's from New York. It just seems odd for somebody down here to marry somebody from New York. It's all right, there's nothing wrong with it. To me, it just seems that we're more old-fashioned than what they are up there." He seemed quite proud, however, of his daughter-in-law's recent display of her spelling prowess. "There was a spelling contest here in Shallotte," he said. "She's a home-health-care nurse, and her company had a team in the contest. She came in third place. I think a lawyer came in first."

The *Irene*

As we roamed around the various docks in Varnamtown and Southport, we discovered a number of men who shrimp in the local waters during July, August, and September not to make a living but for the sheer enjoyment of fishing and supplying their family and friends with a bountiful catch of fresh shrimp. In September of 1991, we ran into one such fellow, Thurman Bass, at the dock at Old Ferry Road.

Retired from the military, Thurman and his son shrimp during the summer in a unique boat named the *Irene*. License number 245329, the *Irene* is one of the oldest boats in the area. Built in North Carolina in 1921 as a clamming boat, the *Irene* was rebuilt from the waterline up in 1980. Thurman purchased the boat, which is 40 feet long, over 11 feet wide, and 4 feet deep, for only $11,500. Powered by a General Motors diesel engine, the boat features two bunks and living quarters below deck. Besides being one of the historical crafts in the area, the *Irene* has the unique feature of a steering wheel located at the back of the boat, as well as one in the small pilothouse. Since he

One of the oldest boats in the area, the *Irene*, built in 1921, owned and captained by Thurman Bass

frequently works the boat alone, and since it does not have an automatic pilot, the rear steering wheel allows Thurman to pilot the boat while working with the nets in the stern.

Suntanned and red-bearded, Thurman looked like the archetypal sailor, a man whose features happily destined him to a watery landscape. He patiently explained all the details of his boat to us and showed us the large needles he uses to mend his nets, the metal TED sewn into his net, the small but tidy pilothouse, and the surprisingly spacious living quarters beneath the deck of his small boat.

The *Cape Fear*

Although the focus of this book is upon the watermen in the area around Holden Beach, we could not resist a visit to the charming town of Southport, which lies about forty miles up the coast. Southport, once a major center in Brunswick County for processing fish and shrimp, still has several busy fish houses and many excellent seafood restaurants on or near the water. During a conversation with the owner of a shell shop located on the dock, we were told that one of the oldest shrimp boats in the area was tied up a few hundred feet away in the yacht basin.

Most of the boats in the basin were sports boats, but two small shrimp boats, docked next to each other, stood out because of their tall masts and outriggers. The *Alice Belle*, with its small pilothouse built low into the bow and its blue nets, was picturesque in the fall sunlight. It is also, we were told, one of the most frequently painted and photographed boats in the area. Built in North Carolina in 1946, it is perhaps the oldest shrimp boat in the county. Well maintained and restored to pristine condition, the *Alice Belle* is still a working shrimper.

While we were examining the *Alice Belle*, Leroy Potter and his son, Royce, appeared on the dock. Leroy explained that he owns and captains the *Cape Fear*, the shrimp boat next to the *Alice Belle*. Born and raised in Southport, Leroy has spent most of his life on the water. Unlike most of the other shrimpers we talked to, Leroy, like Thurman Bass, is not a commercial fisherman. For many years now, he has worked on dredges up and down the east coast, and he had recently become the captain of a dredger for the United States Army Corps of Engineers. While his work takes him away from home for long periods of time, he is always eager to get out on the *Cape Fear* with his son during the shrimping season. Though only twelve years old, Royce is quickly learning the art of the Carolina watermen under the watchful eye of his father.

Built in the 1960s, the *Cape Fear* carries a name made infamous by Robert Mitchum and Robert DeNiro in their movies of the same name. Cape Fear, which juts out into the Atlantic off Southport, is, indeed, a place that over the years has instilled fear into many a mariner negotiating his way through a storm or heavy seas at night. Rather than inspiring terror, however, Leroy Potter's *Cape Fear* links a father and his son in the wholesome business of hard work, quiet adventure, and the promise of a freezer full of succulent shrimp.

What struck us most about the shrimpers we interviewed, both the commercial and the family fishermen, was the joy with which they go about their work. Over a century ago, the

English philosopher Thomas Carlyle wrote in *Past and Present*, "The only happiness a brave man ever troubled himself with asking much about was, happiness enough to get his work done. Not 'I can't eat!' but 'I can't work!' that was the burden of all wise complaining among men. It is, after all, the one unhappiness of a man. That he cannot work; that he cannot get his destiny as a man fulfilled. . . . Older than all preached Gospels was this unpreached, inarticulate, but ineradicable, forever-enduring Gospel: Work, and therein have wellbeing."

Despite the erratic and sometimes punishing economy, and despite the pressures of environmentalists and foreign competition on the shrimper, the Carolina waterman has acquired a well-being that issues out of his long years of hard labor, a work with his mind and body that shapes his biological connection to the world and makes him a model of American independence and self-reliance.

The yacht basin in Southport. *Left to right*, the *Alice Belle* and the *Cape Fear*

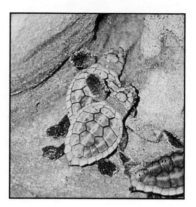

Loggerhead
hatchlings
heading for
the sea

AT LOGGERHEADS
WITH THE SHRIMPER

*A*t Fulford's Fish House, there is a cartoon tacked up on the wall depicting a shrimper and a loggerhead turtle with the caption, "Which is the endangered species?" The humor has a terrible relevance to many shrimpers and their families up and down the Atlantic coast. Already hard hit by the imported-shrimp market, high fuel prices, costly insurance and maintenance for their boats, and a dwindling supply of shrimp due to overfishing and pollution, the Carolina watermen believe that the requirement that they pull TEDs year-round may be the deathblow to their livelihood.

A shrimper that goes out without a TED faces a certain $5,000 fine. A shrimper that goes out with a TED faces the certain loss of 25 percent of his catch. The National Marine Fisheries Service has made it clear that federal agents and the United States Coast Guard will vigorously enforce these regulations year-round for all trawlers twenty-five feet or longer working in the ocean. Smaller boats that shrimp in the ocean and all trawlers that work inshore have the option of using TEDs or limiting their tow time to ninety minutes.

TEDs, which have a trap door to allow turtles to escape the nets and avoid drowning, were developed in the early 1980s when marine biologists determined that trawling was the single largest cause of turtle deaths, an estimated forty thousand to fifty thousand per year in United States waters. Despite the efforts of dedicated groups of turtle-watch volunteers to protect loggerhead nests along the beaches, some scientists believe that the most efficient way to secure larger populations of turtles is to protect the large juveniles and adults that wind up in the shrimpers' nets.

For several years, shrimpers were required to employ the TEDs only during the turtles' nesting season in late summer. In 1991, however, the government, under pressure from environmentalists, required that shrimpers fishing in the Atlantic Ocean use the TEDs year-round. In 1992, federal officials required that TEDs also be used year-round in fishing the inshore waters, such as Pamlico Sound and the Intracoastal Waterway, where three-quarters of all the shrimp are caught. How these new regulations will affect the Carolina shrimpers, already hobbled by inflation and decreasing shrimp populations, remains to be seen.

Jerry Schill, the executive director of the North Carolina Fisheries Association, believes that the new rules are an effort to break the spirit of North Carolina's commercial fishermen. In a letter to the National Marine Fisheries Service, Schill reported that many shrimpers are heading towards bankruptcy or planning to put their boats up for sale. Having represented the hard-working fishermen since 1988, he noted that he had never before witnessed the degradation of spirit that is now spreading among these beleaguered men.

Creatures such as the snail darter, the spotted owl, and the sea turtle have created enormous difficulties for industries and environmentalists alike. The turtle-excluder devices sewn into all shrimpers' nets, however, allow for a grudging compromise between the fishermen and the environmentalists. A look at the loggerhead turtle and the organization that has sprung up to save it from extinction may be helpful in understanding the strong feelings that underlie the controversy.

The Loggerhead

Sea turtles are an endangered and threatened species of marine life. While there are four species — the green sea turtle, the leatherback, Kemp's ridley, and the loggerhead — that make their nests on the beaches of Brunswick County, the loggerhead turtle is the most common visitor.

Female loggerheads, weighing up to 350 pounds, arrive along the Brunswick County beaches in early May through late August to lay their eggs. As the turtle leaves the water on her way to a nesting site, she leaves her distinctive "tractorlike" tracks in the sand. She then digs a pit about eighteen inches deep into the base of the sand dunes with her hind flippers and lays about 120 eggs the size and shape of ping pong balls. Films of loggerheads show them to shed large tears while they are laying their eggs, presumably a biological process protecting their eyes from the sand, but one that gives them an eerie human quality. Once her eggs are laid, the turtle covers the nest with sand and returns to the ocean. The turtle hatchlings emerge between fifty and eighty-five days later.

The hatching process, which usually takes place at night, is known as a "boil." Once the young turtles break through their eggs, they emerge from the pit of sand in what appears to be a small lava flow as they scurry with instinctive urgency towards the light reflected off the sea. As they head down the beach towards the water, some of them are captured and eaten by ghost crabs. Those turtles that make it into the sea are then easy

A loggerhead nesting site

prey for fish. The few hatchlings that make it through these obstacles head towards inland waterways for protection and food during this early stage of their life. They then head towards the Gulf Stream and may travel as far as two thousand miles to feeding grounds. Many of them go to the warm waters of the Sargasso Sea, where they feed upon plants, squid, and jellyfish. Sargassum, a tough seaweed with branches and berrylike air sacs, provides a substantial resting place for their heavy bodies.

It takes about fifteen to twenty-five years for a sea turtle to reach sexual maturity, and it is estimated that only about one out of every seventy hatchlings makes it to adulthood. The males never return to land, but the females return from great distances to lay their eggs at the same beach on which they were born. Scientists believe that during the hatchlings' frantic scurry from their nest down to the sea, they are imprinted with the smell, slope, and temperature of their nesting area. No one knows exactly how the adult female turtles translate this imprinted information into precise navigation back to their birthplace.

The declining population of these marvelous creatures, which graced the warm oceans long before mammals made their appearance on earth, has recently become a great concern to environmentalists. In 1980, the Nature Conservancy and the North Carolina Wildlife Resources Commission established a sea-turtle nest-protection project. Initial attempts to protect the turtle nests were limited to a few devoted environmentalists who patrolled over fifteen miles of beaches known to have nests. Eventually, however, interest in the project grew, and hundreds of volunteers now comb the beaches for signs of turtle tracks and nests.

During the late 1980s, the Brunswick County Parks and Recreation Department established the Brunswick County Turtle Watch Program. Volunteers now monitor turtle nestings at Sunset Beach, Ocean Isle Beach, Holden Beach, Long Beach, Yaupon Beach, and Caswell Beach. Members of the Brunswick Turtle Watch hold permits from the Endangered Species Division of the North Carolina Wildlife Resources Commission that authorize them to monitor nest sites as well as hatchings.

In 1990, the Brunswick Turtle Watch registered sixty-three turtle nests on Holden Beach alone. Thirty of the nests had to be moved to a more secure location because beach erosion led the turtles to lay their eggs below the high-tide mark. There were sixty-seven volunteers on Holden Beach who served as nest patrollers, nest movers, nest adopters, and adopter assistants. There were also numerous visitors who helped lead the hatchlings into the water by shining flashlights in front of them as they made their way from the nests down trenches dug in the sand. The last of the turtle watchers, standing in the surf with a powerful flashlight, directed the hatchlings into the undertow. The count for 1990 on Holden Beach was 3,278 hatchlings that made it safely into the sea.

Visitors to Holden Beach from May to September may notice small areas of sand by the dunes and the steps coming down from the beach houses marked by yellow bands of ribbon. These are the nesting sites marked by the Turtle Watch volunteers. Each site bears a sign stating that harassment of sea turtles, an endangered species, or their nests is a violation of state and federal law and is punishable by a fine of up to $10,000 or imprisonment for up to ten years or both. Most visitors respect the sanctity of these sites and eagerly hope to see a boil before their week's vacation draws to a close. Occasionally, however, mindless violence interrupts the nurturing of the turtle watchers. One moonlit night on Holden Beach in 1991, someone slit the throat of an adult female loggerhead and left it belly up on the beach.

In September of 1991, we participated in overseeing several hatchings on Holden Beach. About ten or eleven o'clock one night, we noticed a flurry of flashlights several houses down from us and joined a small group of excited people awaiting the boil. A trench had been carefully dug from the nest to the surf to facilitate the first and perhaps most important journey of the hatchlings' lives, the one that was to imprint the location of their future nests. The turtle watchers busily answered questions from the visitors about the loggerheads as they kept an eye on the nest. They had counted the days and believed that the boil would be tonight. A few crumbs of sand would move, everyone would grow excited, and then nothing would happen for a half-hour. Some of the visitors grew bored and cold and drifted away. One man who had obviously been drinking too much grew impatient and kept repeating that he would like to reach down into the nest with his hand and "get them turtles going." From that point on, a watchful eye was kept not only on the nest but also on the too-eager spectator.

We were interested in the talk of the turtle watchers themselves. These volunteers had learned a great deal about the loggerhead during the previous few years they had been active in the program. They had read the writings of Archie Carr, a marine biologist who spent his life studying the sea turtle, and they were ready to answer most of the questions visitors put to them. What struck us, however, was not the scientific data they had acquired but the language they used in describing the turtles. Mostly women, they expressed a strong maternal feeling about their charges. The words *mother* and *babies* used to describe the turtles were spoken with a certain passion. These women were accustomed to sitting in the sand dunes next to the nests into the wee hours of the night.

The strength of the turtle-watch program lies in part in the bonding of the volunteers and visitors who gather around the nests. We found ourselves caught up in the excitement of the boil as we eagerly walked along the edge of the trench with our flashlights, lighting the way for more than eighty hatchlings as they waddled with untrammeled determination towards the sea. Occasionally, one of the turtles strayed out of the trench, and we picked it up and placed it back on its path to its watery home. Moving its flippers as quickly as it could, leaving small herringbone tracks in the sand, it headed towards the flashlight of the woman in the surf who counted out loud the number of each passing turtle. The thought crossed our minds that by touching the hatchling, we were imprinting our smell upon its memory and were possibly confusing its future navigational sense. On the other hand, better that than allowing it to go off towards the waiting claw of a ghost crab. It was an adventure to be a part of this mysterious cycle of the loggerhead's life, and we came to respect the efforts of the Brunswick County Turtle

Watch Program to help preserve this endangered species.

Although there are several known threats to the survival of the loggerhead turtle, no one threat appears to account for its declining population. In earlier times, the turtle was hunted for its eggs, shell, and meat. Nineteenth-century sailors used to stow live turtles in the ship's hold for fresh meat. Some people used to gather turtle eggs in the belief that they were an aphrodisiac. In more recent times, turtles have drowned in shrimpers' nets, been shredded in dredging operations and slashed by boat propellers, and been poisoned by tar or choked by swallowing plastic bags mistaken for jellyfish. Erosion and development along the beachfront have added to the turtles' struggle to survive. The bright lights of beach houses and businesses along the coast disorient the hatchlings, leading them away from the water, towards land and certain death. In addition to all of these obstacles, of course, are the numerous natural predators, such as birds, fish, and crabs, that feast upon the newborn turtles.

The most visible predator of the loggerhead, however, is the shrimper. Unlike the careless boater who tosses a plastic bag into the water or the beach-house renter who leaves his house lights on during hatching season, the shrimper has been singled out by some as the archenemy of the loggerhead as he ruthlessly drowns turtles in his nets during his quest for shrimp. Some sportfishermen have joined in the attack upon the shrimpers, claiming they are killing many prize game fish.

Unlike the sportfishermen, who have a powerful organization that lobbies the government for regulations favoring their activities, and unlike the turtle-watch organizations that are spreading along the east coast, the shrimper is now paying dearly for his years of independence. Lacking a vigorous social or political organization, the shrimper must content himself with venting his frustrations with his fellows at the local fish house. He complains when waters are closed to his shrimping, when industries pollute his waters, when federal and state agencies require that he learn CPR and carry expensive safety equipment, when foreign shrimp are allowed to be imported in record numbers, and when the government demands, upon heavy penalty, that he pull TEDs year-round.

In many respects, the shrimper is like the small farmer. Independent and hard-working, part of the economic backbone of America for decades, both are now being driven out of their livelihoods by new economic, environmental, and corporate forces. Nurtured during the time of a simpler America, when the land and sea repaid their self-reliance and hard labor with a bountiful harvest, the small farmer and the shrimper now find themselves facing an economic wasteland not of their making.

Most of the shrimpers we talked to stated unequivocally that in twenty or thirty years of shrimping, they had caught only a few, if any, loggerhead turtles in their nets. In most cases, they simply jumped on the back of the netted turtle to drive the water from its lungs and returned it safely to the sea.

Conscientious shrimpers are perhaps more concerned with the environment than are the turtle watchers. After all, their very livelihood depends upon clean waters that bristle with life. They are quick to point out that the loggerheads were not threatened by shrimpers in the past, that it was only with the development of the coastline with factories, businesses, and beachfront residences that the problem began to surface. Under the pressure of devastating fines, however, they pull the TEDs, knowing they are losing hundreds of pounds of shrimp and hundreds of dollars each week.

Most of the shrimpers we talked to referred to the turtle-excluder device as a "turtle shooter," because it is constructed so as to "shoot" the turtle back into the sea through an opening in the shrimp net. Wycuff Skipper, a welder and the manager of a fish house, vented his frustration by writing the following poem in 1991, shortly after the announcement that TEDs must be pulled year-round:

> Our rivers are dying from toxic wastes,
> Our environment from air polluters.
> Now they're trying to starve the shrimpers to death
> Making them pull them turtle shooters.
> I wish the man who dreamed them up
> Had to wear one on his tail.
> Let's change his plan
> And try to preserve man.
> Take his TED and go to hell.

Skipper, fortunately, has his welding business to sustain him, but as someone who has worked closely with beleaguered shrimpers for years, he shares their frustrations and vents it in his homespun verse.

Shrimpers happily coexisted with sea turtles for decades, and it is only now, with the environmental pressures of beachfront development and pollution, that they must face the unpleasant consequences of powerful forces beyond their control. Every time the shrimper goes to work, he must see and handle the TEDs sewn like some grotesque, alien transplants in the coherent webbing of his nets. They stand for him as a daily reminder of the mortality of his profession.

Other Bycatch

Anything caught by fishermen other than the intended species is called bycatch. The loggerhead, because of its dwindling numbers, has become the most notorious bycatch associated with shrimpers. In recent years, however, other species of discarded marine life caught in the trawl nets have washed onto the beaches, causing a strong reaction among environmentalists.

The North Carolina Division of Marine Fisheries estimates that the average shrimper catches four pounds of bycatch for every one pound of shrimp. There are no hard data, however, to support these figures, and the bycatch fluctuates depending upon the season and location. Shrimpers usually have the largest bycatch in the late winter and spring, when fish come inshore to spawn.

Commercial shrimpers are not the only ones who contribute to this problem. Sportfishermen will throw back a catfish, skate, or other species not to their liking. With more people fishing every year, the problem is growing worse and is drawing the attention of fisheries managers.

In an attempt to address the proliferation of bycatch, the North Carolina Division of Marine Fisheries mandated that beginning in October of 1992, finfish-excluder devices (FEDs) be installed in the tailbags of all trawlers working in coastal waters. Finfish-excluder devices are stainless-steel rings sewn into the nets to create small openings through which fish can escape. The holes are positioned to keep the weaker-swimming shrimp from getting out.

Jim Bahen, a marine-advisory agent with the University of North Carolina Sea Grant Program at Kure Beach, argues that FEDs make shrimpers more productive than before. By allowing the fish to swim free, shrimpers can tow their nets for longer periods of time. The FEDs also give the fishermen a better product, he says, because they reduce the weight of fish in the tailbag, which can crush the delicate shrimp.

Fisheries officials also argue that besides saving fish, a reduction in bycatch will make shrimping a more efficient operation. When a full shrimp net is dumped on the deck of a boat, the first thing the crew does is put the shrimp on ice. Marketable fish such as flounder and whiting are pulled out next, while the rest of the catch is left to die and is pushed overboard for sharks, birds, and other scavengers to feed on. The smaller the bycatch, the easier it is for the crew to gather the marketable species.

Sportfishermen applaud the new restraints placed upon commercial shrimpers, who, they believe, are destroying many of the species of fish they are seeking. They point to a recent study that indicates that at least fifteen species of fish are either stressed or overfished.

A report published by the Gulf and South Atlantic Fisheries Development Foundation, however, points to the impact of new regulations upon the commercial shrimper. It states that factors such as unwanted TED regulations, escalating costs, and foreign competition "have combined to cause extreme concern among shrimp fishermen that bycatch management may impose additional and potentially insurmountable hardship on their way of life."[1]

The plight of the commercial shrimper is an acute one. He is a victim of a changing economy. Before the development of beach resorts and sportfishing, no one would have noticed a bycatch washed up on the sand. With the development of beach and golf resorts along Holden Beach, Ocean Isle, Long Beach, and Southport, however, the area has become increasingly affluent. Along with that affluence have come hundreds of individuals eager to fish the Atlantic and the waterways in their powerboats. Competing for a common and limited resource, the sportfishermen and the commercial shrimpers have, sadly, become antagonists. Money and influence clearly favor the sportfishermen. The shrimpers, whose families have happily worked the waters since the turn of the century, must now improvise in order to survive hardships their parents never dreamed.

---

[1] The *Brunswick Beacon* (July 23, 1992), 11c.

THE FISH HOUSE

Fulford's Fish House

*T*he fish house is the place to be. Anyone who visits Holden Beach who wants a sense of the life that has been going on there for over a hundred years ought to stop by one of the several fish houses within an easy mile or two of the beach. There are four fish houses that take in most of the shrimp and fish caught by local fishermen: Honey's Place, at the end of the road in Varnamtown; Fulford's Fish House, at the end of Old Ferry Road; Capt'n Pete's Seafood House, under the Holden

Beach bridge on the south side of the Intracoastal Waterway, actually on Holden Beach; and Bellamy's Fish House, on the north side of the bridge. Three of these establishments are readily visible when one crosses the Holden Beach bridge (Capt'n Pete's is too close to the bridge to be seen). Just look for the cluster of shrimp boats that regularly tie up next to them.

Honey's Place, Fulford's, and Capt'n Pete's are the most accessible places to visit. With luck, one might see a shrimp boat being unloaded or the women gathering around the long table to dehead shrimp with a speed and precision that comes from years of experience. At quiet times or during the days they are closed, one can usually walk out on the fish-house docks and discover several local people fishing from the docks or the anchored shrimp boats.

Although the obvious function of the fish house is to take in, prepare, and market seafood, it is also the place where local residents, workers, and fishermen gather to talk. These people make the fish house a vital social center. Shrimp-boat captains and their crews can be found here working on their docked boats or just hanging out, discussing their mutual problems, such as the TEDs. Reluctant at first, they are willing to talk to strangers and can relate some fascinating stories. It was at Fulford's Fish House that we first met Henderson Caison and his brother Charlie. They were talking about the dollar bills they had caught in their shrimp nets. Charlie had recently netted a twenty-dollar bill. They believed the money was thrown into the water by people on the party boats. It seemed more mysterious to us. There are also several local residents who have been coming to the fish houses for years just to while the time away, be with other people, and pass on some local gossip.

Fulford's Fish House

Goodman Fulford

In September of 1990, we talked to Goodman Fulford, who started Fulford's Fish House around 1950. A tall, slender man sporting a NAPA cap, he sat on a bench next to us and rather laconically related the story of his early years. He occasionally punctuated his words by spitting tobacco in a can he kept nearby.

"I was born in 1916 and raised a little up the road," he said. "It was nice, peaceable back then. You could lay down anything and you could go back and it'd be where you left it. Nobody locked their doors and nobody locked up nothing. But now, you better lock your door even if you're inside.

"I remember when there wasn't a building over there," he continued, referring to Holden Beach. "I remember the first building was built right straight across over there, where the old pavilion's at. My daddy built it. It was called the Old Hotel. They had several rooms upstairs and downstairs. They sold drinks and candy, had a cafe there and a place where bathers could change clothes. I think they rented the bathing suits then for a nickel or a dime.

"I was here before the Waterway was ever dug in. There was an old bridge coming across a little old creek—a little old wooden bridge—marshes all around. You could drive across the bridge, but you couldn't go any further. There was a big, white sand hill—just as white—and you couldn't drive anything across it. Just pure, clean, white sand.

"As a boy, there wasn't much to do unless you lived on a little farm and raised things. You could always go to the beach, pull a boat in June, and look for turtles.

"I mostly fished for mullets and spots until I got married in '39. Always self-employed, except for about six months I worked in a chemical plant before I was married. A little after I got married, I came on out here and had me a retail market for a good while. And then two fellows out of Wilmington built a fish house, and I operated it for four or five years before I bought it. I've been running it ever since."

We asked him if he had seen any changes in the business, and he laughingly replied, "From bad to worse. The production's way off. We used to get a whole lot of fish and shrimp. The biggest problem is there's too many people after them. That's what I think. There are so many boats now. One boat they got today would equal a half a dozen of the boats back yonder when it started out. Back then, you just had small boats with car engines. Now, all of them got big rigs. You used to pull one net, and now they're pulling four. And the shrimp is just not there. And they work summer and winter, seven days a week, and they just don't give the shrimp a chance to multiply. Back then, they didn't used to shrimp until the first of July, and then about Thanksgiving everything was over. Now, they do it year-round. Not all of them. It gets too dull, or some of them quit or move to Florida.

"We got four right big trawlers working here now. Sometimes, we might have five. Then again, they might move up to the sound for a week or two or go south. Some of them will move to South Carolina or Florida in October. All of the shrimpers that work here live within a two-mile radius."

Most of the fish brought into his house have been caught with gill nets. Mullets and spots are the most important catches in the area, although some flounder and whiting are also brought in. Most of the snapper, he says, come in at Southport. Fish such as snapper and grouper are caught on electric reels in about two hundred feet of water.

Although he has sold some of his shrimp and fish to Northern companies, most of it is sold locally. "We get buyers in here," he explained, "mostly from the county or maybe the adjoining counties. A lot of them will come in and buy a few hundred pounds for their market, or maybe some of them will peddle them. Later on, when the spots start running, there'll be a truck in here about every day, and they'll take all they can get. There'll be a big wholesale man, and he'll take them back, and what he don't sell he'll freeze for the off-season."

Goodman estimated that the average catch for a good four days of shrimping is about ten to fifteen boxes, 100 pounds to the box, deheaded. "Most I ever unloaded off one boat—about fifteen years ago—was 9,813 pounds." He spoke those numbers slowly, indelibly etched as they were in his memory.

"My son, Freddie, just put in a freezer," he continued. "He's going to freeze some stuff this year. He's already frozen some shrimp. I gave the business to my son about six years ago. But I'm here as much as I ever was." Freddie was not at the fish house during our visit, but we met him later. Asked if his son enjoyed the work, Goodman replied, "Well, it's all he knows. He's been in it ever since he could fish through a crack in the fish-house floor. I had to pull up the planks to get his fish in."

As we listened to Goodman, it became clear that he embodied a past that was at odds with the present. The old fish house reverberated with ghostly memories of a different world that he vividly recalled for us: "I spent some long hours in this business. It's a gravy train now. This is what you call a gravy train to what it was back then, when we started. You didn't have no conveniences. You didn't have a telephone. We did have electric lights. You had to haul all your ice from Wilmington or Shallotte. You had to crush it by hand. Finally, we got a grinder. The road here was a dirt road. Those fellows from Wilmington were in it in a big way. They had closed-in trucks, tractor trailers, to haul the ice down here.

"Our children wouldn't believe it if you were to tell them all this. They wouldn't understand it. Now, we make our own ice, we got a telephone, we got a ship-to-shore radio." Referring to the men at sea on the shrimp boats, he said, "I can call one of the boys anytime and talk to him. Even the small boats that bring in the fish have radios.

"It's been hard work. At times, it's been too much work. To go back to where I first started at — sometimes I think about it — the amount of hours we used to pull. The boats didn't come in until sunset, and then we had to do all this deheading until we got through, maybe eleven, twelve, or one o'clock at night. Now, we close the doors about 6:30 P.M. and go on home. Back then, hardly any boats came in by the time we close now. Of course, now they don't work the whole week."

As we were completing our talk, a harbor dredge passed by the fish house, causing Goodman to recall again what it was like to be here in the 1930s, before the Intracoastal Waterway was dredged. We then walked out on the dock to take a photograph of him. He looked rather jauntily at the camera and said, "I hope you finish this book in a hurry. I'm getting old."

When we returned to visit Goodman in the spring of the next year, we discovered that he had recently died. His son, Freddie, was working in the fish house with a group of women deheading a huge pile of shrimp that had just been unloaded. We watched him wash the shrimp, ice them down, and put them into his new freezer, and we wondered if he ever thought of his business as a gravy train.

Bellamy's Fish House

Thurman Wycuff Skipper, known to everyone simply as Skipper, is the son-in-law of Norman Bellamy. He began working in his father-in-law's fish house and welding shop in 1975. The welding shop was a part of Bellamy's boatbuilding

Wycuff Skipper, welder and part-time manager of Bellamy's Fish House

establishment, but when he stopped building boats about 1985, Skipper took over the welding business and expanded it to include a variety of work besides rigging boats. He has been managing the fish house since 1986, but since it is only open during the shrimping season, about four months of the year, Skipper spends most of his time in the welding shop. He is responsible for unloading the boats and seeing to it that the shrimp get deheaded. His wife, Quintina, actually arranges for several women in the town to come to the fish house to do the deheading upon the arrival of a boat. Skipper then oversees the washing, boxing, and icing of the shrimp. He stores the packaged shrimp in his cooler and arranges for various companies to buy them. "It's not a complicated thing," he explained. "Almost any idiot can do it."

We first met Skipper in September 1990 when he was overseeing the unloading of the *Capt. N. C. II* at Bellamy's Fish House. He was too busy at the time to talk, so we visited him again in November of the next year. It was a quiet Sunday morning, and we sat on a bench in the doorway of the fish house facing out onto the Waterway.

"Now, we have only two boats come in here," he said. "We had as many as six in the past. But all those boats began to interfere with my welding business, so I told Mr. Bellamy that I would take care of his boats and my brother-in-law's boat, but the rest of them would have to find another place to go." The *Capt. N. C. II*, Norman Bellamy's boat, and the *Miss Becky*, Skipper's brother-in-law's boat, regularly bring their catch to the fish house now.

Billy Smith, Skipper's brother-in-law, is the captain of the *Miss Becky*. Billy's brother, Carleton Smith, who owns the boat, had been working with Western Union for twenty years when he suddenly lost his job in management. Since he was from the Brunswick County area, he decided to buy a shrimp boat and try his hand at making a living on his own. One of his deck hands had been working for NCR for fifteen years, and when he lost his job, he also turned to shrimping.

The *Miss Becky*

The *Miss Becky* is one of the few rib boats that can be seen in the area. It was built in 1968 by St. Augustine Trawlers, a Florida boatbuilding company, which, like Desco, another Florida boatbuilding company, built rib boats for years until the declining shrimping industry caused it to go out of business. Although the *Miss Becky* is much larger than the rib boats that John Varnam was building decades earlier, the design and construction methods are essentially the same. To an untrained eye, the *Miss Becky* and the *Capt. N. C. II*, a timber boat, look similar when they are in the water. Seeing them on the railway in dry dock, however, one can immediately see the difference between the two boats. The ribbed construction of the *Miss Becky* gives it a huge, rounded, deep hull, whereas the exposed hull of the timber boat shows it to be sleeker and more sharply sloped to its keel.

As we were talking about these two boats, an old man asked Skipper to help him find something he needed. The man was W. C. Evans, who owns three shrimp boats: the *Sea Robin*, the *Miss Evans*, and the *Molly Ray*. His son, Jeff, runs the *Sea Robin*, which was built by Norman Bellamy. Mr. Evans captains the *Miss Evans*, built by Billy Varnam, and someone named Jim captains the *Molly Ray*, also built by Billy Varnam. We asked Mr. Evans if he had ever eaten a rock shrimp. "Now, I'm gonna tell you something," he replied. "Them rock shrimp are good. Between a shrimp and a crab is what they taste like. But they're hard to clean." He explained that rock shrimp have to be caught way out at sea. We told him that we often saw his boats going along Holden Beach, and he said, "The inlet back to the pier, we call that 'The Graveyard' because there've been so many nets hanged on rocks and old wrecks between those points." He then headed off to go fishing.

Skipper admitted that he had never been shrimping himself, except in a small, twenty-one-foot boat in the canal. "I've been a part of building shrimp boats for twenty years and have never done any outside fishing on one of them like these boys do. I've built the rigging, fuel tanks, anything metal on the boat, but I've never gone out on one."

The amount of metalwork on a shrimp boat is considerable. The mast, the outriggers, the winches, and the elaborate system of cables must work smoothly together and support an enormous amount of weight. With a ballpoint pen, Skipper attempted to trace on the fish-house floor the network of cables that gives the shrimp boat its characteristic silhouette. We easily followed his drawings while he explained how the hold-back cables that run from the outriggers to the bow support the great tension on the outriggers during dragging, but our grasp of the system began to fail during his attempt to trace the system of cables involved in dragging four nets.

Skipper's welding work also involves repairing the huge fuel tanks in the hold of the shrimp boats, as well as refurbishing the propeller shafts, propellers, and rudders of boats that have been damaged by rocks. All of the metal parts of these boats must be kept painted to protect them from the corrosive seawater to which they are constantly exposed. Eventually, however, metal fatigue and corrosion bring the older boats under the restorative hands of Wycuff Skipper.

Besides managing the fish house and running the welding shop, Skipper has been making poems in his head for years. He wrote some of them down for the first time in 1992. Sitting on the bench in the fish house, looking out towards the water, he recited one of them for us:

Ode to a Possum

While riding through the scenic South
Amidst the trees and blossoms,
The one thing I'm concerned about
Is all them road-killed possums.
We got laws protecting turtles
And laws for bear and deer.
But will the possum be extinct,
A fate I sorely fear?
What can we do to help protect
Our furry little friend?
Put possum guards on every car
And watch them possums grin.

Although Skipper laughed at the conclusion of his recitation, beneath the humor of the verse lies a deep-felt resentment against the federal regulations requiring TEDs to protect the loggerhead turtles from being caught in the shrimpers' nets.

Skipper then recited a poem about "all you move-in's down here," a nostalgic account of the Edenic days of Holden Beach:

I Remember When and Bet You Can, Too

I remember when there weren't nothing over there
And now it's full of mobile homes and folks from everywhere.

And I remember when you could sit and rock all day.
Only traffic you would see was the mailman on his way.
And I remember when you didn't have to lock your house.
The only unwanted visitor was a rat snake or a mouse.
And I remember when men would tip their hats and smile
And wonder what in the world was going to become of
   ladies' styles.
Dresses past their ankles and then up past their knees.
And now they're up past places where we shouldn't ought to see.
But time goes on and things do change and I've lost more than
   just my hair,
But I can still remember when there weren't nothing over there.

Finally, Skipper looked at us earnestly and said, "Now, here's a serious poem. This one I made up while riding down the highway. It just came to me."

Ode to a Highway Sign

Darling, let's sit down and talk
And maybe say a prayer
About something very special,
Something we both can share.
I know now it's impossible
To have one of our own,
But we need that special something
To make our house a home.
So I've checked in with foster care
And this is our lucky day,
For first thing in the morning
We can adopt our own highway.

A colorful character with a lively mind, Skipper not only helps to keep the shrimp flowing into the marketplace and the shrimp boats' rigging in tiptop shape, but his clever playfulness with the language makes him one of those special people who might otherwise go unnoticed among casual visitors.

Capt'n Pete's Seafood House

Capt'n Pete's Seafood House, owned by Pete Singletary, is the most comprehensive fish house in the Holden Beach area. Whereas the other fish houses are essentially wholesalers of fish and shrimp, Pete combines a wholesale with a vigorous retail operation. From early spring until Thanksgiving, visitors to the island mingle with residents to buy locally caught fresh seafood. Crabs, flounder, red snapper, pink snapper, gray snapper, sea bass, shark, shrimp of all sizes, and spots are among the

Capt'n Pete Singletary,
owner of Capt'n Pete's Seafood House

many offerings. The staff happily explains how to prepare any of the unfamiliar seafood and cleans and fillets the fish for the customer.

In addition to selling seafood, Pete provides supplies for the fisherman, including bait, tackle, ice, and gas. He also leases his dock to accommodate three charter fishing boats and a boat that takes visitors on a scenic cruise up to Southport. In 1989, he added onto the fish house a very large gift shop that sells clothes, nautical items, and ice cream.

Pete's highly successful operation, unique in the area, is a testimony to his intelligence, hard work, and intuitive understanding of the changing times. A shrimper for most of his life, he purchased the fish house in 1980, when he sensed it was time to get out of shrimping. Within a decade, he established himself as one of the foremost entrepreneurs in the area.

A large, powerfully built man in his fifties, Pete usually wears a hospital scrub top. He has bright reddish hair and an engaging accent that must be heard to be appreciated. He has two daughters — Rita, a nurse, and Opal, who works at the fish house along with her husband, Jesse. Rita's husband, Travis, also works at the fish house, as does Pete's wife, Augusta, who usually tends the cash register.

Pete was born in his grandparents' house, located about a mile and a half from his business in what is now called Varnamtown. The house has since been moved to another location, but every time Pete drives past the empty lot, he stops and looks at it. He has lived in the area all of his life, except for a year in Philadelphia when he was in the first grade, the two-year period when he was in the army (1954–55), and the short time after he left the service, when he worked for Babcock and Wilcox in Florida. "I always wanted to get back to the water," he explained.

Pete's love of the water derives from his grandfather, who fished all his life. "He used to ride me all around the river," Pete said. "I was on a shrimp boat for the first time when I was about twelve years old. When I was in the tenth grade, I was fairly robust for my age, and I hired on to fish for menhaden." He fished out of one of the two seine boats that surround the menhaden with the seine net, which is then pulled up by a third boat. It was physically exhausting work, but he enjoyed it, and it enabled him to purchase his first automobile.

It was during this time that his grandfather taught him a lesson he was never to forget. "One day when I was a young boy," he recalled, "my grandfather said to me, when I was a little slow getting ready to fish, that the saying 'Time and tide wait for no man' wasn't completely true. He said that *nothing* waits on you. When you think about it, it's true — nothing waits

The *Amor*, docked at Capt'n Pete's Seafood House

on you. And that's the way I was thinking when I was shrimping later on in life. I was better off heading south to shrimp than I would be lying around the docks up here. If you don't catch them shrimp while they're there, you'll never catch them." The work ethic was firmly planted in his mind, and years later it proved to be most valuable.

All of the shrimp boats that Pete owned and worked were built by Weston Varnam. The first one he purchased was a fifty-foot boat called the *Black Eagle*. It was about twelve years old when Pete bought it in the mid-1960s. He ran it for a while and finally paid it off. "The boat is still running out of Wrightsville Beach and is renamed the *Eight Ball*," Pete said. "It's in good shape. I like to see it come by. When I was shrimping, I didn't have to look — I could tell every boat by its sound, by its motor. Anyway, I sold the *Black Eagle* and bought the *Earl Lynn*, a sixty-five-foot boat, from Preacher Weston. I worked it until he made me the *Amor*."

When Pete ordered this last boat, he got one larger than he expected: "When Preacher started making that boat, I told him that I wanted it to be seventy-five feet at a maximum. One day, he came by and said, 'Well, Pete, the boat's going to be a little bigger than we thought it was. It's going to be about seventy-eight feet.' A few days later, Preacher came by and told me it was going to be a little bigger still. He finally got it up to eighty-one feet."

It took Weston and his brother Ed a little over a year to finish the boat. "I helped some during the day," Pete said, "but they didn't hurry any. They showed me what to do so that I could help with some of the heavy work. They're amazing people to watch build boats."

Pete did all of the steelwork on the *Amor*. He built an A-frame with towers on it that enabled him to move the heavy rigging onto the boat. "Preacher helped me put the engine in," he explained. "Now, he's an engineer! You give Preacher and Ed a crowbar, and they'll move the world. We raised the mast by hand, every bit of it. We put a block-and-four onto it and raised it up into a cradle to hold part of it. Then we got five men around the booger and raised it right up. We did all this down where Betty's Restaurant is now."

Back in the forties and early fifties, the fish house was just a small shack that was owned by several members of the Caison family, who were relatives of Pete's. Then Hurricane Hazel came through in 1954 and destroyed it. The Caisons went over to the woods where some homes were being built, gathered some lumber, and rebuilt it. "They continued to run it until the 1960s, when my brother-in-law bought it from them," Pete explained. "Mr. Goodman Fulford one day asked him how much he was going to pay for it, and he answered, 'Five thousand dollars.' Mr. Goodman then said, 'I durst declare, a fool and his money are soon parted.' My brother-in-law kept the fish house until 1980, when I bought it from him. What I paid him was a big difference from what he paid for it."

During the first several years, Pete ran the fish house and got somebody to work his boat, the *Amor*, during the summer. When September came, Pete got on the boat himself and shrimped his way down to Florida as the weather got colder. He and his crew lived on the boat during these trips away from home. At Christmas time, they tied up the boat in the Gulf and returned home to be with their families. Then they returned to the Gulf and continued working until the shrimping season opened up back home. Most of the shrimping they did down there, they did at night. The water is so clear that the shrimp bury themselves during the day to avoid predators. At night, they come out to feed, and that is when Pete caught them.

Back in the Carolina waters, Pete would anchor his boat at night so as not to disturb the white shrimp. Although it had been several years since he last went out shrimping, he fondly recalled some of the details: "That's the best sleeping in the world, out there on a shrimp boat, after you've been working

Deheaders working on shrimp

all day. We had three bunks and a couple downstairs we never used. No washing machines. We'd take our clothes, tie them on a line, and throw them over the back of the boat. The wheel water beats them pretty and clean. We'd take them in and rinse them in fresh water. Cotton clothes came out very soft. One time, we threw out our clothes on a line and forgot to pull them in. They got under that wheel water, and by the time we pulled them in, they were beat all to pieces."

We asked Pete if he ever ran into any female shrimpers. "There are no women shrimpers down here," he said. "There used to be one in Southport years ago. Now down south, in the Gulf, there was a boat that was all women. I don't think they really shrimped that hard. They went around buying shrimp from other boats. They would buy them at half-price and take them in and sell them."

Pete also explained a more significant economic twist within the shrimping industry: "Some years back, when shrimpers were making good money, many people were attracted to the business—lawyers, doctors, farmers, people with no experience. The federal government was willing to give low-interest loans to people inexperienced in commercial fishing so that they could buy boats, but experienced fishermen were denied such loans. Everybody in the world got into the business. That's what helped these shipyards grow around here. But it was worse in Texas, Louisiana, and Florida. They overfished the area. And all these inexperienced fishermen told the banks, 'Here are your boats. We're through.' You could almost name your price for these abandoned boats. Now, the business has gotten back to the real fishermen. The doctors, lawyers, and farmers, meanwhile, got a big tax write-off on their 'losses' in shrimping."

Pete is gradually turning his business over to his children and their husbands. He has given his daughters the opportunity to do whatever they want in life. Both of his daughters have gone to college. Rita chose to become a nurse, while her husband, Travis, her sister, Opal, and Opal's husband, Jesse, decided to expand the fish house. While Pete continues to handle the seafood operation, Opal, Jesse, and Travis place most of the orders and have been instrumental in modernizing the establishment.

"We don't do anything extravagant," Pete declared. "We love to camp and relax." Besides Capt'n Pete's Seafood House, Pete owns some oceanfront apartments and some property on the mainland that he hopes to develop. Known during his shrimping days as "Hog" because of his large appetite for food, Pete also has an insatiable appetite for hard work. As his grandfather taught him, nothing waits on man, and Pete's fierce dedication to getting back to the water and riding the shifting tides in order to survive and prosper and provide for his family has made him a quintessential waterman. His idea of relaxing during his camping trips to Florida and to the mountains of North Carolina is to spend his days fishing.

Hammering down the planking on the bottom of a shrimp boat

THE BOATBUILDERS

The Varnam Family

*O*ver a hundred years ago, a man named John Varnam introduced the building of shrimp boats to Brunswick County. His sons and their families carried on the tradition of boatbuilding through most of the twentieth century and established their preeminence in crafting high-quality wooden boats at a reasonable cost. We spoke with two of John Varnam's sons, Weston and Clyde, both in their seventies, and with his grandson, Billy, who is in his fifties. It quickly became apparent to us that we could best understand and appreciate their mastery of boatbuilding by knowing something of their family history, since these men learned their craft from their fathers.

Located near Lockwoods Folly River about a mile away from Holden Beach is a small community named Varnamtown. Although the Brunswick County telephone book lists the names of over thirty Varnams and fifteen Varnums, the actual number living in and around Varnamtown is obviously much larger. Many of the listed residents have several people in their households, and many of the female Varnams bear their husbands' names. There are so many Varnams in the area that most of them have no idea how they are related to each other. Some of the Varnams, however, have begun to investigate their history.

In 1957, a woman named Martha Varnum Stayner printed a seven-page history of the Varnum family based upon her research of records in Maine and Massachusetts. She sent the history to "all my Varnum relatives who are interested in their ancestors." Among the details of her report, she noted that the first Varnums came to Ipswich, Massachusetts, in 1635 from Drawcutt, near Wiltshire, England. The first Varnum on record in Maine was Matthew Varnum, born in 1758. It is from Maine that the Varnam boatbuilders trace their family line.

Weston Varnam gave this account of how his family arrived in Varnamtown: "My grandfather, Roland Varnam, came from

Portland, Maine. He went up the Cape Fear River to Black River and married an Indian girl. They had six sons—Sam, Roley, Billy, Jim, John, and Dave. They lived for a while on an island in the Cape Fear River. Then they moved to Howells Point, or somewhere in the area. My grandfather died and was buried there.

"When my father, John, was a small boy about ten years old, and his brother Dave eight, they walked to Southport from Howells Point to where their brother Sam was living at that time.

"While he was there in Southport, he went down to the waterfront, where a man called Mr. Manuel had a boat shop. He went in where the man was working, and Mr. Manuel asked my father if he would like to come live with him. My father did not have anyone to look out for him at this time, so, at the age of ten, he moved in with Mr. Manuel. He then went to work cleaning out the boat shop and learning about building boats.

"Sometime later, they moved to Wilmington, and Dad stayed with Mr. Manuel until he died. He then moved to Varnamtown and started to build shrimp boats. He built them for many years, and it followed in the family.

"My father had five sons—Johnny, Hoyal, Clyde, Eddie, and Weston—and all five sons are boatbuilders. My brother Johnny has a son, Billy Varnam, who owned a boatyard called the B-Var Boat Yard, and my brother Hoyal has a son and son-in-law, Harold Varnam and Richard Heil, who own a boatyard. My brother Clyde was the first to own a boatyard. N. C. Bellamy owns one which branched out of the Varnam boatbuilding."

When we later talked to Clyde Varnam about his family, he added to his brother's account by filling in some colorful details about his grandfather, Roland: "Our grandfather—he came from Maine—came down here on a sailing schooner to Wilmington. There were some Galloways who lived over at the river who at that time happened to be at Wilmington. Grandfather went over to one of the bars they have—a-setting in there and drinking—and old man Galloway told him come up to see him over Lockwoods Folly River. Grandfather came back—I guess he left the ship—and he came on out and went over to Lockwoods Folly River. And he got up with Mr. Galloway and he stayed over there. I don't know how long. He sold his boat and bought a small boat with a sail on it. He came out of Lockwoods Folly River and sailed up the beach to Cape Fear. He went up Black River and got married to an Indian girl named Sarah Pridgett. And he came back down out of the inlet, out of Cape Fear, to Lockwoods Folly over the river, and he stayed there until he died.

"All the children they had are dead and gone. My father was one of them. He got married, and in his first boatbuilding he worked for a man in Wilmington. Then he came out here and started building. And down at the end of Varnamtown, over in a field, he used to build boats. The last one he built was at Riverside. At that time, they called that area Wild Cat. The last boat he built was in 1933. He built it for a fellow in New York named E. C. Squires. The boat burned up one night. I don't know what happened, but the fire burned the side of an old white oak.

"In fact, it's still standing down there," Clyde concluded, as he pointed out the window to a tree about fifty feet from his house.

All of John Varnam's boats have long disappeared after years of hard use and the ravages of sea worms and time, but the scarred white oak and the memories of his sons mark a quiet memorial to the man who shaped a generation of boatbuilders. Born in 1869, John Varnam died in 1949. He was sixty-four years old when he built his last shrimp boat, the only one that never reached the water.

WESTON VARNAM

Weston Varnam and his wife, Mary, live in a modest ranch house on Brown's Landing Road (recently renamed Stone Chimney Road), about a mile from Holden Beach. A few blocks away, at the end of Old Ferry Road, are a dry dock and fish house where he sometimes steals a few

Weston Varnam

afternoon hours to relax and talk to the fishermen bringing in their catch or having their boats cleaned and repaired. Now in his mid-seventies, Weston has spent most of his life as a waterman, having worked first as a shrimper in the Gulf and along the southeastern coast and then, during the past several decades, as a boatbuilder and carpenter in Varnamtown.

"I've built most of the houses in this neighborhood," he said, "and I've got one I'm working on now." Most of these houses were built for his family and relatives. "I never made money from the houses I built," he said. "I got a pocketknife and two ducks for the house I built for my nephew." Known among the local residents as "Preacher," Weston has also kept active as a Baptist minister since his ordination in 1951, at age thirty-two.

Mounted on a wooden frame over the entrance to his driveway is a large model shrimp boat that he built some years ago. Expecting to meet a large, burly man, we were surprised when we saw Weston sitting at the end of his driveway in a lawn chair awaiting our visit. A small, wiry, soft-spoken man about five foot seven, Weston seemed an unlikely person to have captained two large shrimp boats out of Texas and Key West, to have built over a dozen shrimp boats by himself, and to have worked with his brothers on over fifty other boats.

Weston showed a great pride in his family's history of boatbuilding. A natural teacher, he visits the local schools in his spare time to talk to the children about shrimping and boatbuilding, so that they will have some knowledge of their heritage. He showed us several scale-model shrimp boats he built for his friends, some of which he takes with him to the schools in order to illustrate his talks. The outriggers, nets, doors, and winches on these models all work in much the same manner as they do on the actual boats. He then brought out a large-scale model net and laid it out on his driveway in order to explain how it works. Apparently, we were not the only ones impressed with his clear explanations of shrimping and boatbuilding — Weston has received two plaques from the state of North Carolina, one signed by the governor, for his public service in keeping the watermen's heritage alive in the schools.

Weston began by explaining the differences between the boats his father built and those that he and his brothers built: "There is quite a difference in the boats my father built from the ones we build now. A boat they build today would have taken my father two years to build. The boats Dad built were much smaller in size. The biggest was about forty feet long, twelve feet wide, and about three feet deep, with a round hull. The cost of it was between three to four hundred dollars.

"The material my father used to build them was one-by-two, twelve-feet-long oak strips called ribs, which made the framing. He had to steam them so that he could bend them to make the shape of the boat. He'd start a fire under a tank of water, and the steam would go up into the steam box and soften the ribs. He'd take the ribs out while they were hot and limber and press them upside the boat. Then he'd plank her and tear the strips off her, and she was ribbed. Then he'd get in there and put the deck things into her and bolt them and the ribs and what they call a chine plank to hold it tight, and then he'd deck it over.

"One-inch material was used for planking and decking, and two-by-sixes for deck beams and floor timbers. He used number-eight square nails and number-eight galvanized round nails. The boat had a six-inch keel put together with three-eight rod iron cut up for fastening.

"In the boats that are built now, timber boats, when you have the framing up, you don't have to bend any ribs. They put the planking to the framing and bolt the floor timbers through the keel lumber. The bolts are sixteen inches apart, and two bolts go down through the keel holes down into the keel and the floor timbers all the way to the stern. The framing is four-by-eight, deck beams are four-by-twelves, planking is two inches thick, and decking is two inches thick. They are double-planked inside, ice bins are fiberglassed, and the keel is twelve inches wide. They use number-twenty, sixteens, eights, and sixes stainless-steel nails. The bolts are twelves, tens, eights, seven-and-one-halfs, and sixes, all by one-half and three-fourths, and five-eight rod iron.

"Some boats today have freezers, air conditioners, electric stoves, gas heat, two bathrooms, television, stereo, radio, electric pilots, radar, Lorans with plotters, radio telephones, washing machines, and dryers. The cost of a boat today runs from $100,000 to $450,000."

Weston also noted that his father built all of his boats entirely by hand. He did not have the luxury of power tools. "He had what they call a drawing knife," Weston recalled, "and he'd work the planks out with it. His other tools included hand planes, handsaws, a two-foot rule, chisels, six-inch clamp screws called C-clamps, a hand brace, a few bits, a hacker, a level, a hatchet, and a hammer." Today, he observed, boatbuilders are equipped with such tools as power saws, chain saws, electric sanders, power hammers, electric drills, ten- and twelve-inch C-clamps, beam clamps, electric planers, saber saws, and radial-arm saws.

The fishermen working out of John Varnam's round-bottom shrimp boats during the twenties, thirties, and forties had to work harder than the fishermen today. "They used flat nets,"

Weston explained, "that ran anywhere from fifteen to fifty-five feet. The doors to spread the nets were made out of boards ranging from two to five feet in length and from fourteen inches to thirty inches in width. They used leads on the nets to hold them down and corks to hold them open." Unlike modern shrimp boats, however, these older boats had no winches. "The catch was pulled in by hand," Weston continued, "unless they had too big a catch. Then they had a bail net to bail the catch out of the net onto the deck. They had no try net, and many of the boats did not even have a mast. All the work was done by hand."

Without modern electronics and without a try net, the shrimpers of that period depended exclusively upon their experience and good luck to locate the shrimp. Most of their boats were powered by jerry-rigged automobile engines. A few boats had Chrysler marine engines. Otherwise, if a man could afford one, he installed a Lathrup or Palmer engine with anywhere from 12 to 40 horsepower! Modern shrimp boats, on the other hand, are equipped with large diesel engines that range from 250 to 500 horsepower. Nevertheless, the fact that the largest annual catch of shrimp recorded in Brunswick County was in 1945 suggests that the unsophisticated boats of the old-timers were more than adequate to their task.

Although only in his young twenties when he came to what is now called Varnamtown, John Varnam had mastered the fundamentals of boatbuilding during the years he worked with Mr. Manuel in Wilmington. "The people in the area," Weston explained, "got my daddy to build shrimp boats. Now, I won't say my dad was the first one to build shrimp boats here. Once in a while, somebody else would build one, but not like Dad's and not as many. The older boys — Johnny, Hoyal, and Clyde — learned building from my father, and Eddie and I then worked with them together. My brother Clyde built the most boats, but everyone built some. That's how the Varnam boatbuilding got started."

With the exception of Billy Varnam, the boatbuilders we interviewed have not kept any records of the boats they built and cannot account for their whereabouts today. Many of their boats, however, can still be seen docking at the local fish houses or dragging off the area beaches. Some are hundreds of miles away working along the coast of Florida or in the Gulf. Treated roughly, a few have fallen into disrepair or have sunk.

Fortunately, one of Weston's boats, the *Andrea Dawn*, was bringing in a load of shrimp to Capt'n Pete's Seafood House at the time of our visit. Eighty feet long, the *Andrea Dawn* (formerly the *Amor*) is larger than the typical shrimp boat. It was hard for us to imagine how this massive boat was built by a man not much bigger than the boat's rudder.

"I built the *Amor* for Pete Singletary about ten years ago. It was the last boat I built. I built it out in the yard here, between that house and here," Weston explained, pointing to his neighbor's house. He said this as if he were describing a place where he had planted a small rosebush, but we were hearing Noah explaining that he had constructed his massive Ark in a suburban neighborhood. Brown's Landing Road is a quiet street with woods running along one side and manicured lawns and modest ranch homes on the other. The idea of an eighty-foot shrimp boat gradually emerging between two of these homes was rather startling to us. We had imagined that these boats were constructed in huge metal sheds in an industrial section of town.

We asked to see the plans he used to construct the *Amor*, and Weston explained that he and his brothers never used any plans. All he needed to know was how long, wide, and deep someone wanted his boat, and he would proceed to build it. His only concern was not to make a miscalculation that would make it difficult to fit the shaft into the hull or that would leave the engine sitting too low. His tools housed in a small garage, Weston completed the construction of the *Amor* within a year. After installing the shaft, rudder, and keel cooler, he had some men put the boat on a trolley, haul it along the highway, and put it in the water in Varnamtown. While it was tightening up in the water, Pete Singletary put in all of the rigging—the mast, outriggers, and winches—along with the fuel tanks and the Cummins diesel engine.

The first boat Weston built was called the *Black Swan*, which he completed in 1948. "I named it after a pirate gunboat that had a hundred guns onto her," he said. "I saw it in a movie years ago." The motion picture was a 1942 swashbuckler named *The Black Swan*, starring Tyrone Power as the pirate who wins the heart of Maureen O'Hara. "I imagine it's gone now," he said of the boat. "I sold it to a man in Florida who made a party boat out of it. Then I went to Piedmont Bible School in Winston-Salem and came back home and attended the Fruitland Baptist Bible Institute from 1952 to 1955.

"After I finished Fruitland," he continued, "I built the *Black Eagle*. It's called the *Eight Ball* now. I also built the *P.J.*" He laughingly explained that the letters stood for "Puddle Jumper." For Weston, the naming of boats was important, sometimes playful, and always creative. "Now, it's called the *Track Down*," he said. "Both of them are still running. They're good little old boats."

The naming of boats is always a special occasion for their owners or builders. Some conjure up romantic images derived from legend, motion pictures, or television, such as *Sea Dragon, Black Swan,* and *Drag Net*. Others refer to creatures associated with the sea, such as *Albatross, Octopus, Squid,* and *Black Fish*. Others still, such as *Bug Hunter, Black Eagle, Predator, Scorpion,* and *Track Down*, depict the boats as hunters. Perhaps the most creative name among all the boats we have seen is the *Amor* (now the *Andrea Dawn*). When Pete Singletary purchased that boat from Weston Varnam, he managed to come up with a name that not only included the names of his wife, Augusta May, and his daughters, Opal and Rita, but one that also expressed his love (amour) for them and for his livelihood as a waterman.

Weston recalled a few other boats he built: "I also built the *Bug Hunter*, the first V-12 rig ever around here. Then I built one called the *Earl Lynn*. I named it after my two children. Diane Lynn's my daughter and Earl's my boy's name. Then I built my son-in-law and my son one, the *Scorpion*. They wanted another one, so I built another, the *Capt. Scott*, named after my grandson. They're still working those boats, and I get all the fish and shrimp I want from them."

In recollecting the past, Weston expressed a quiet satisfaction in the fact that he was able to help others without a profit motive: "I worked almost all my life for nothing. How I done it,

I'll never know. I worked as a carpenter for five years and got paid for it. I also worked during shrimping season down at Cedar Landing with my brother on boats for a while and got paid for it. But I've worked half my life for no pay. And I've been preaching for about forty-two years, and half of that time I charged nothing. The Lord has taken care of me. My house is paid for, my car and truck are paid for."

Weston seemed rather resigned to the fact that no one in Brunswick County is building shrimp boats any longer.

The *Bug Hunter*, built by Weston Varnam

"Boatbuilding from Maine to Texas has just about come to a close," he remarked. "All of them down in Florida, as far as I know, have gone out of business."

The rising cost of labor and materials, he explained, makes it impossible to build and sell wooden boats nowadays: "I built two boats about twenty-one years ago. One year, I bought a V-12 diesel and it cost $12,200. The next year, it cost $12,400. Today, it costs $40,000. You can't afford it. Along then, you could. You could get cypress lumber then for $100, and now it costs $600. You could get a hull for $100 a foot. Now, it costs $1,000 a foot. If you built Pete's boat today, it would cost you $90,000 just to hull it. The engine, $40,000." He said that Billy Varnam has built some boats that cost $350,000.

Weston recalled that his years as a shrimper placed even more physical demands on him than boatbuilding: "I've been up to Pamlico Sound and started fishing Monday morning and not shut her down until Wednesday. Come in, refuel, unload my catch, and go right back out and not shut her down until maybe the weekend. Just two of us. We didn't sleep all day. It fatigued us to death. I got too old. I haven't fished for years."

Nevertheless, he fondly remembered the rich harvest of his nets: "Crawdads, spots, whiting, stingrays, sharks, eels, tonguefish, toadfish, croakers, Virginia mullets, flounders, conch shells, and seahorses. We'd keep the fish if they were over thirteen inches long." He showed us his collection of seashells, displayed in a lighted curio case in his house. Among the items were delicate shapes of white coral, two seahorses, large lion-paw shells, and several olive shells. Many of these shells he caught in his nets while shrimping in Florida and in the Gulf.

He obtained some of them from other shrimpers.

Fishing in the Gulf, he explained, is different from in North Carolina: "Down there, you don't catch the fish and trash you do up here. Down there, the shrimp are pink. The bottom's white sand. Here, it's black mud. Some of the shrimp down there are what they call Royal Reds. About 16 of them will weigh a pound. You catch them offshore. If you fish closer to the beach, you catch smaller shrimp running anywhere from 31 to 35s to 80-count. Biggest I've sold is 16 to 20s. They used to sell by the bushel. Way back then, they sold for $1 a bushel. I fished them at $5 a bushel. Now, they get over $100 a bushel."

Weston is now enjoying his retirement from shrimping and boatbuilding. As he says, "My son's got a shrimp boat. My son-in-law's got one. I built their boats. They're in Georgetown, South Carolina, now. All I got to do is tell them to bring me some fish. My brother's son is working at the dry dock in Varnamtown. He's a young fellow, a little fellow smaller than I am. I sometimes sit on the porch down there. It's cool, nice, and passes the time away some."

He also passes the time away in building model shrimp boats. Besides the several models he keeps in his house and the one at the entrance of his driveway, he showed us a large model, four feet long and four feet tall, housed in his garage. This meticulously constructed boat, fitted with outriggers, pulleys, and nets that actually work, was mounted on a small trailer decorated with Christmas tinsel in preparation for its entry in the September Varnamtown Parade and the October Festival by the Sea. Another of his models may be seen in the Varnamtown fish house called Honey's Place.

When we visited Weston the following year to pick up a model boat he had built for us, he took us into his study to see "the fleet." There, on a long table, were ten shrimp boats in various stages of completion. Blue, orange, red, and white, these precise scale models sparkled with fresh paint. He lowered the outriggers on one of them to demonstrate how the pulleys and cables worked. Here, on one table, Weston had conjured up in miniature the many shrimp boats he had built for his family over the years, and each one looked as handsome and seaworthy as the real thing.

In addition to his work as a shrimper and a boatbuilder, Weston was the pastor at Sabbath Home Baptist Church for ten years, at the Gospel Center in Varnamtown for fourteen years, and at Mt. Olive Baptist Church in Supply for eighteen years. Although he claimed to be retired from the ministry after over forty years of preaching, Weston continued preaching for several years on Sunday nights at First Baptist Church in Shallotte.

Some of his fondest memories are of a trip he made to the Holy Land a few years ago: "Oh, mercy, that's something to behold. Golden sand. Looked like Holden Beach before it was developed. As far as eyes could see, golden sand." He took over four hundred color slides in the Holy Land, which he has shown in local churches. He visited the pyramids in Egypt, where he became interested in the hieroglyphics: "I didn't know much about that because I didn't have the privilege of learning that in school." He then visited the tomb of Jesus, followed the trail of Moses, and crossed the Sea of Galilee. "I'd love to have a boat in the Sea of Galilee," he remarked. "I was baptized in the Jordan River. Since I was already baptized, it really didn't do me no good. I just wanted it done." This trip to the Holy Land seems to have given Weston a realization of his kinship with the fishermen who, like him, also preached the gospel.

CLYDE VARNAM

Clyde Varnam

We first met Clyde Varnam in March of 1991, about six months after we spoke with his brother Weston. His house, which was up for sale when we visited, was located on the Intracoastal Waterway, almost in the shadow of the bridge connecting Holden Beach to the mainland. A few feet down the road were the home, fish house, and dry dock of Norman Bellamy, another prolific boatbuilder. Clyde's house, however, stood out from all the others in its delightful Dickensian eccentricity. To please his wife, Addie (now deceased), who enjoyed fishing, he had the rear of his house built like a boat deck extending out to the Intracoastal Waterway. Coming off the deck, an added structure leading into his kitchen was curved and windowed like the pilothouse of a shrimp boat.

Several inches taller than Weston, Clyde is a powerfully built man whose large, calloused hands tell of the decades of sawing, carrying, and hammering lumber. There were no signs in his robust appearance or movement that he was in his late seventies. Occasionally pulling off his navy cap to run a hand through his full head of white hair, Clyde recounted many fascinating details about his work as a boatbuilder.

He related the story of how his father came to the area and began building round-bottom boats, and how he learned the trade by working with his father. "The first boat I worked on," he said, "was the one that my father built and that burned up in 1933." He laughingly explained that "along then, you know, I had girls on my mind. They'd come down and we'd go swimming."

Several years passed before he settled down and began building boats on his own: "I started building in 1947. I worked about two or three years before I moved down here, about 1949. Before that, I lived on the edge of Varnamtown, about three miles from here. When I first started building, I'd haul the boats to the river. I made a trailer to haul them on. I welded two automobile chassis together and would haul the boats on them. But the boats got larger and larger. Along then, we were building about forty-two-foot boats. You could haul them, but whenever they got up to around forty-eight feet and then right up to ninety feet, you couldn't haul them."

And so, with the demand for larger boats, Clyde moved to a new location where his boats could more easily be launched. "We built a track here to the water," he explained, "to launch the boats. We built a track of cement and put railroad iron into it and launched the boats on that."

He described in detail how he went about building his boats: "There were eight of us who built these boats. The five of us brothers and my brother-in-law, Charlie Caison, worked together. And Billy Varnam worked with me for about fifteen years. His daddy worked with me for twenty-four years." Billy Varnam is Clyde's nephew.

"It's hard work," Clyde continued. "In the summertime, we'd work ten hours a day. It was interesting work, you know. You take a deck plank — three by ten, twenty-two feet long — that you got to hold one end of, one man at the other end. You have to pick that thing up under the strip and hold it and catch your clamp screw until they bolt it. When the day's work was over, you knowed you had been to work.

"We used heart pine for the framing. When I first started, you could get what they called longleaf heart pine. It takes them probably a hundred years to grow up. But in the last of the boatbuilding, we used what they called loblolly pine. They'll grow up in about twenty-five years. The longleaf pine is a thing of the past. And we used cypress lumber for the outside and the

The men who worked with Clyde Varnam in 1954. *Left to right, top row:* Eunice Fulford, Rev. Gracie Varnam, Clyde Varnam, Calvin Hewelle, Wilbur Caison. *Left to right, bottom row:* Hoyle Varnam, Johnnie Varnam, Unknown, and Ed Caison.

inside of the boats, the heart pine for the decking. We used two-inch planking on the inside and out. I bought my cypress from E. E. Gothin, a Wilmington lumber company. I bought some from Red Springs. I bought some heart pine from a fellow named Blake in Southport. He had a mill in Orton Plantation and cut a lot of heart pine. But I bought most of my lumber from Gothin because he saved all the heart pine and cypress he could for the boatbuilders. At the last of it, there were about four places down here building boats that were buying from him. It took a lot of lumber. If you plank a sixty-five-foot boat on the inside and outside, it takes ten thousand feet of lumber.

"To start with, we used double-dipped galvanized nails. In later years, we used stainless-steel. They cost ten cents apiece if you bought them by the pound. We got them cheaper by buying them by the keg—about $200 or $350 a keg, for about a hundred pounds.

"I used glue on the small boats, the ones we built out here in the shed, such as houseboats or small party boats, about thirty or thirty-five feet long. We'd put glue on the frame but put the planking up there and still nail it. But we didn't use glue on the larger boats.

"After we got a boat built and painted with a white, oil-based marine paint and ready to launch, we'd put one coat of copper paint on the bottom, and then we'd go over it with beeswax that had been boiled in copper paint. It would make a putty, and you would take that and put it in the seams. You'd go over that with a second coat of copper paint and then launch the boat. If you let that copper paint stay up for a while, it will die, turn to powder. The least thing will knock it off. After you put copper on her, you have to launch her within a week. Then you would tie the boat up over here on the dock for a day or two until the wood swelled and the planks come together, shoving out the beeswax putty.

"I built a boat for a fellow named Thomas, and he was there when we launched it. We turned the thing loose, and it went down there and busted the cradle and turned over. Someone said, 'That's the way to launch them.' And Thomas spoke up, 'That's a hell of a way to treat a boat!' We would bust a cradle once in a while and the boat would fall over, but we never hurt one.

"Caulking cotton would leak in about three years, turn dark and rot. We didn't caulk our boats. All we caulked were the butts. And we didn't even caulk the butts in the last boats we built, because we put a pin in the butts instead.

"We built boats with two propellers, and we built them with one. If the boat's sixty to sixty-five feet long, we'd put a V-12 in it, or one of them big Caterpillars. If you take care of that engine, it'll last a long time.

"The boats we built had keel coolers in them that allowed fresh water to circulate and keep the engine cool. We used rubber packing around the outside of the keel cooler to make it watertight."

When he first started building boats, Clyde had the rigging done by someone named Miller at Shallotte Point. After Miller went out of business, Norman Bellamy, Clyde's next-door neighbor, rigged all the boats. He installed the mast, outriggers, engine, fuel tanks, and hoists. Norman was also one of the major boatbuilders in the area.

We asked Clyde how many boats he had built over the years. "Now, that's a little hard for me to say," he answered. "One time, I sat down and tried to figure that out, because I didn't keep any records of the boats that I built. The number I came up with was 133. Mostly what we built were shrimp boats. Later, we built all kinds: head boats, party boats, cabin cruisers, and sportfishermen's."

Somewhat baffled by government regulations concerning the building of party boats, Clyde sometimes worked under the watchful eye of federal and state inspectors: "Now, for a party boat, you couldn't go over sixty-five feet in length. The government man would come out of the customs house in Wilmington, and he showed you where to put each bulkhead — you had to put bulkheads on them — and it couldn't be over sixty-five feet long. If it was two inches over sixty-five feet, it would come under a different classification. I didn't know what it all meant, but what we did was keep them just under sixty-five feet. I don't know how many people you can put on a sixty-five-foot boat, about fifty, maybe. You had to have two bathrooms and a place to take care of the fish and things like that on them. But the boats we built were good. The government inspected them."

All of his boats were custom-built to the specifications of the buyer. Some were used for rather mysterious purposes, and others traveled to the other side of the world: "One of the boats I built was sent over to pick up some people in Cuba, and it had to be built in a certain way to do that. I built it for a man named Captain Weathers. He was out of Marathon, Florida. He made two or three trips to Cuba to bring people back here. And I built a shrimp boat that went to the Persian Gulf. We had to build a cradle for that boat to set in. They took it to Charleston and put the cradle on deck and picked the boat up. I don't know what kind of ship it were, but I understand it were a German ship."

He also built clam dredgers, rather awkward-looking but efficient instruments for harvesting clams: "You'd build a barge, and it'd have a frame on the side that would be lowered to the bottom of the water. Pipe went down that would blow the clams out of the water, and they'd come up on a conveyor belt. There'd be clams and shells together, and they'd have a couple of men up there picking the clams out while the shells went overboard back into the water."

With the decline of boatbuilding in the mid-1980s, it has become increasingly important for fishermen to follow a vigorous program of maintenance for their old boats. Docked next to Clyde's house was one of his old boats, the *D & E* (now named the *No Way*), a fifty-foot trawler which from a distance still looked bright and healthy. We later learned that the captain of the *No Way*, Gerald Pittman, Sr., age fifty-five, drowned after he was lost overboard near the Long Beach fishing pier in July 1992. Then in March of 1993, the *No Way*, grown fragile over the past several decades, started taking on water at its dock near the Holden Beach bridge. It was moored next to another vacant trawler, and the boats hit against each other. Holes were knocked in the *No Way*, causing it to go down by the stern and keel over slightly to its port side. Unable to pay to raise the boat and clean up the oil spill, the owner abandoned the *No Way* to the Coast Guard, which towed it away. As far as we could

No Way, built by Clyde Varnam
© Copyright, the *Brunswick Beacon*

ascertain, this was the only remaining boat in the area built by
Clyde Varnam.

Docked next to the *D & E* was the *Miss Caison*, which Norman
Bellamy built many years ago for Clyde's brother-in-law,
Charlie Caison. One time, Charlie apparently left his boat in
the water too long, and he and Clyde had to perform some
necessary surgery on her: "Me and my brother-in-law, we've
done a right smart of work on the *Miss Caison*. Worms got into
her and we had to put plank into her, but that's been some years
back. They'll last pretty good if you take care of them and if
they're built out of stainless-steel nails. You have to clean the
bottom good and paint it with a couple of coats of 'Forty-nine.'"
"Forty-nine" is the name for copper paint. "Then it would be all

right to leave them in the water for six months," Clyde continued, "though they should be pulled every three months. If you don't take care of them, they won't last no time. I reckon most of the boats I built, the worms have already got."

Clyde was philosophical about the demise of boatbuilding. He turned his business over to his son-in-law in the 1970s. "I kept telling them boys that were still working on boats that boatbuilding was going to die. I told them probably a year before it did. You take interest going up, fuel going up, and less shrimp—there ain't no chance for it. Shrimp-boat building is a thing of the past." Reflecting on the damaging effects of inflation, he observed that "when I was building boats, you could buy an engine for about $8,000. Now, it costs you about $35,000 for one of them V-12s. The first boat I built when I came here was a forty-eight-foot boat that I sold for $2,500. For years, I built for $100 a foot—a sixty-five-foot boat cost $6,500. I furnished everything and the labor. At the last of it, I charged $155 a foot. But to have one built now, it would cost you about $1,200 a foot. And that's just for the hull."

When we asked him why some shrimpers have gone into other businesses, such as running restaurants or taking tourists out on pleasure cruises or sportfishing expeditions, he replied, "They have to. Nowadays, these shrimp boats are tied up all along the river. One thing that messed up shrimping this year was that freeze we had last year. The canal up here froze over. Sheets of ice came floating by this house. Well, you see, that killed the shrimp. That's what ails it now. The shrimping is just about a thing of the past. You could probably go over there now and buy all the boats for what one used to cost you. By the time you built her, got it rigged and ready to go to sea, you probably could buy just about all them boats that are over there. There are a lot of boats now that are on the market, if a man wanted them. But if he can't make no money with it, he got no use for it, for there's a lot of upkeeping on the boat."

Sitting across from Clyde at his kitchen table, we kept wondering all the time he was talking what he must be thinking. Here was a man whose life's work had slipped quietly into history. His 133 boats, which rode the waves from the Persian Gulf to the Atlantic, each had a unique life of its own, providing its owner with a good livelihood. Many were eaten away by sea worms. A few still work the Southern coast, and others, unknown to him now, continue riding on distant waters. Surely, he must be nostalgic about these wooden children, these Pinocchios of the sea. We asked him about this, and he said, "When I finished a boat, I tried to forget it just as quick as I could!"

BILLY VARNAM

The son of John Varnam, Billy Varnam represents the third generation of Varnam boatbuilders. A robust, barrel-chested man in his fifties, Billy sends off sparks of energy when he is either talking or working. A life of hard physical labor, combined with a set of genes from a family of long-livers, has kept him very fit and youthful. To shake hands with him is much like putting one's hand in a large vise, which, fortunately, he does not close to the breaking point.

After Clyde moved from Varnamtown to his location on the

Intracoastal Waterway to build his boats closer to the water, his four brothers worked with him. Young Billy followed his father to work and hung out around the boatyard to watch his uncles and father magically turn piles of lumber into sleek hulls of shrimp boats. "Uncle Clyde let me put putty around the seams and cracks," Billy recalled, "just to keep me occupied. He never tried to teach me how to build a boat, because it's something that just can't be taught."

After he got out of the service, Billy worked a few years at a mill in Wilmington, but his love of the water quickly brought him back to the Holden Beach area and to boatbuilding. In 1966, he set up his own boatyard, named B-Var, located on the Intracoastal Waterway at the end of Old Ferry Road. The first boat he built was a fifty-one-footer, the *S. W. J.*, for a man named W. A. Tompkins of Supply, who named the boat after his three children, Sherry, Wayne, and Jeanine.

Like his father, Billy realized that if he had a poor year as a boatbuilder, he better have something to fall back on. Although

Billy Varnam and Sugar

his father was a boatbuilder for over fifty years, there were times when there was no boat to build and he went to sea as a crew member of a shrimp boat. In 1975, Billy also found himself without much work, and he and a cousin, who jointly owned a shrimp boat, went to sea. "I'd rather build a boat than shrimp," he said, "but I don't mind it so much. We'd go out on Monday morning and come back in on Wednesday, working eighteen hours a day. Then we'd go back out Thursday and come in on Saturday." Having built shrimp boats for years, it seemed only logical to captain one of his boats and actually shrimp for a while. "Most people we sold to already own boats," he said, "and wanted me to build a commercial fishing boat. We added a percentage to the cost of materials and labor and gave the buyer a custom design."

During the 1960s and 1970s, the work crew at B-Var consisted of Billy, his father, his brother-in-law Vernon Lewis, and his first cousin Eldred Robinson. All of the timber — cypress and heart pine from Wilmington — was shaped in "Grandpa's way," by hand. The eighty-five-foot *Walter Daphne*, for example, contained sixty-one thousand feet of lumber — excluding the deckhouse — which the four men had to haul, clamp, bolt, and shape by hand. Because heart pine became increasingly difficult to obtain, Billy occasionally salvaged high-quality wood from old buildings to use in his boats. Most of the rigging for his boats was handled by Norman Bellamy.

"When a Varnam builds a boat," Billy said, "all he needs to know is the length, width, and depth that a customer wants his boat to be. I would ask the customer what size wheel he wanted to turn, so that I would know how to stack the keel to keep it high enough for the propeller to miss the bottom of the boat. I might sketch the boat on the back of an envelope. I remember once showing a government inspector a three-inch sketch on an envelope and he just cussed." We asked him if he ever used a blueprint, and he jokingly replied, "I don't think there's a Varnam smart enough to read a blueprint."

Billy sometimes becomes animated in describing the building of a boat. It is almost as if he is creating a new life: "On the first day we lay the keel, I feel excited about how she's going to look. The keel, that's the backbone of the boat!"

He went on to describe a detail of construction unique to his boats: "You have the keel timber—that's the timber that bolts to the keel—and you have the floor timber that bolts to the keel timber, and you have the uprights that bolt to the floor timbers.

The inside of the bow of a shrimp boat

The way I build them, I put still another brace between the uprights and the floor timbers for added strength. I may be the only one that still does that.

"The reason I put the brace in there is as follows. We made a round knuckle where there used to be a square chine. We started making them round to make it look better, and in order to do that, when you were cutting a round in it, it would cut the floor timber and the uprights so nearly in two that you had to put another piece in it. I got to looking at that and thought that here's an ideal place for strength. And now, no matter how I build them, that way or with a round, I still put that brace in there."

Despite the many splices necessary to the construction of a timber boat, Billy asserted that it is clearly a stronger boat than the unspliced rib boats that his grandfather used to build. Pointing to the boat he was building in his backyard, later named the *Predator*, he said, "In this boat here, every turn and center is put together. You'd say the rib boat would have to be stronger because it's not spliced. But it's not. That boat there will tear a rib boat all to pieces." One of his boats, he went on to say, will last forty years or more, depending on how it is cared for. When properly handled, his shrimp boats will even survive severe storms: "She'll withstand weather most anywhere you go. If you were out there in a bad blow, she might get beat to death unless you let her bob like a buoy. Then she'd have you beat to death, but she'd keep on going."

The appearance of shrimp boats gives some clue as to where they were made. Holden Beach boats—those built by the Varnams and by Norman Bellamy—are characterized by high gunnels, square sterns, and rounded pilothouses. The boats that were built up the coast at Harkers Island were high at the bow, with low gunnels, rounded and low sterns, and squarish pilothouses.

Billy has built well over forty boats since he started in the business in 1966. Ranging in length from thirty-five to ninety-six feet, most of them are still shrimping in waters from New Jersey to Brazil. "The last shrimp boat I built, the *Capt. David*," he said, "I started in 1981. That's when the business dropped out. The fellow I was building it for, we had to quit on him. And he'd get a little money and we'd work on it again. I finally got it launched in 1984. That was the last shrimp boat I launched when I was in that business."

It was the launching of the *Farmer's Daughter* in 1980, however, that will always stand out in Billy's mind. A crowd of about fifty people gathered at the B-Var Boat Yard to watch the launching of this magnificent 91-foot-long, 125-ton shrimp boat. Custom-built for Ralph Hewett of Shallotte and Key West at a cost of $350,000, the *Farmer's Daughter* was completely fitted with mast, outriggers, engine, and the latest in sophisticated electronic gear. The boat was pulled down the launch ramp by another shrimp boat, the *Capt. N. C.*, piloted by Henderson Caison.

Billy recalled what happened then: "When they pulled it off the ramp and it hit the water, they had the quadrant jammed so that the rudder couldn't fly one way or the other. When it hit the water, there was a little bit of vibration, and the chocks fell out, causing the rudder to turn and drive the boat into my pier. After she hit the pilings, she kept sliding and turning. The other

Molly Ray, built by Billy Varnam in 1968, in dry
dock for cleaning and painting

boat kept pulling her with the towline high up at the mast. It
was pulling her now in the same direction as she was rolling
over, and the current was falling to help pull her over. With the
outriggers all on her up there in the air on a light boat, the
situation got to the point that no one could overcome."

The four workmen aboard during the launch escaped
unharmed, but the sparkling white boat continued taking on
water until it capsized and lay on its side in some ten feet of
water, its mast and outriggers completely submerged. The
water flooded the engine and destroyed all of the electronics.

The story, however, had a happy ending, as Billy explained:
"The state was repiling the swing bridge at Holden Beach at the
time. I had a cousin working for the state then, and he called

Raleigh, and they brought a crane down here and got a diver to hook a line to the mast. They uprighted the boat, and we pumped it out. It cost the insurance company $100,000.

"The engine in the *Farmer's Daughter* was running until it smothered itself out in the water. It was underwater no more than twenty-four hours before we got it back up. As soon as we got it pumped out, we called the fire department up here. We let all the oil out of the engine, and they washed everything out, inside and out, with fresh water. Then we put new oil in the engine and cranked it back up before it had time to freeze up. We had to replace the electronics and rewire it, but there wasn't any damage to the hull. That boat fishes now around St. Augustine and the Gulf."

Such freak accidents are rare among the Varnam boatbuilders. This was the only time a boat capsized during a launch, and the Varnams launched several hundred boats during the past hundred years. Attracted to the ceremonial launching by the

The *Farmer's Daughter*, on its side in ten feet of water

great size and beauty of the *Farmer's Daughter*, the onlookers were treated to an unscheduled spectacle that was both exhilarating and sickening.

Several months after the *Farmer's Daughter* was on its way to Florida, Billy completed building his largest shrimp boat, *Big Mama*, which ran ninety-six feet in length. He built several other boats during the 1980s, but inflation and the decline in shrimping gradually brought an end to shrimp-boat building in the area. Billy was one of the last to get out of the business.

After he closed down the B-Var Boat Yard, Billy took all of his tools and lumber and put them in a large shed in the back of his house, located across the street from where he had the boatyard. "I got cleaned out twice down there," he lamented, "so I brought all my stuff up to my house and work out of a shed in my backyard."

It was in his backyard that we first met Billy in September 1990. Weston Varnam, Billy's uncle, joined us as we drove to Billy's house to take a look at the party boat he was building there. While we were talking to Billy, Weston, with the enthusiasm and energy of a boy, climbed the ladders rising up against the hull to inspect the construction. "That boat," Billy said, "is the sixth one I built right there, in my backyard. Last year, we built two fishing boats there. One of them was sixty-two feet long. This one is forty-two feet long." When we stopped in to see Billy in the spring of the following year, he had completed the party boat, which was named the *Predator*.

Although he has a son, Brent, who is in his twenties, Billy declared that "when I turn up my toes, the boatbuilding will be over." We asked him if his son was interested in carrying the

Varnam tradition of boatbuilding into the next century, and he laughingly replied, "Brent thinks a hammer is something to throw away.

"There'll still be plenty of boats built," Billy continued, "but they'll be blueprint and fiberglass. The craftsmanship will be gone. As far as the way my family built boats and the way that a boat is built through a blueprint is as different as black from white. You take two carpenters, a boat carpenter and a house carpenter, and it's hard for them to interchange. The advantage they have is they know how to use tools. But boatbuilding requires working with angles. Houses are built on plumb and square. The principles of how to go about boatbuilding, those will be lost."

Back in 1976, Billy was quoted in the *Durham Herald* as saying, "The best name for this place is Scuffle Town. See, we have to scuffle to get by. Yes, sir, that's a good name for it." Billy has proved himself to be adept at scuffling. After twenty years of successful boatbuilding at the B-Var Boat Yard, he built a restaurant on that property. Managed by his wife, Betty's

The *Predator*, completed in 1991

Seafood Restaurant is the only restaurant in the Holden Beach area that fronts on the Intracoastal Waterway. Although he occasionally works on repairs to the restaurant, Billy still spends most of his time in building pleasure boats in his backyard.

Billy is the only Varnam boatbuilder who has kept a record of all his boats. A list of the forty-three boats he constructed between 1966 and 1993 is in the appendix on pages 175–76. Several of his boats may still be seen in the Holden Beach area. Others are working off the coasts of other states, and a few are trawling in foreign countries.

Norman Bellamy

Norman Bellamy

Norman Bellamy was the next-door neighbor of Clyde Varnam for several decades. About forty yards from Norman's former house, his boat dock and fish house remain fairly active. When we first visited him in September of 1990, several shrimp boats—including his boat, the *N. C. II*—were tied up, ready to unload their catch. The remains of his boatbuilding yard, including the launching tracks, still stand next to his house. Now in his seventies, Norman has sold his business and his house on the causeway and has moved into a house he built for himself about a mile away from the water.

"I was a building contractor to begin with," Norman explained. "I also shrimped dead-ahead for two years up and down the coast, to the Gulf of Mexico and up around the east coast to Pamlico Sound. Then I started boatbuilding in the 1950s. In the summer, I would build boats, and during the winter, I would build houses. I began by remodeling a boat, and then Weston Varnam helped me to build my first boat in 1958. That boat, the *Capt. Troy*—it was originally called the *Miss Island*—is still around here. The owner is Jerry Caison. It works mostly out of Georgetown, South Carolina, which is a six-hour run down the coast here."

During the next twenty years, Norman and his workers built over fifty boats. One of his boats burned up, but all the rest are still in the water. Like the Varnams, he never used blueprints in constructing his boats: "I had plans for a commercial trawler. I had plans for a pleasure boat. I built both kinds, but I never built the first pleasure boat by the plans, and I never built the first shrimp boat by the plans. Everybody had

The *Capt. Troy*, the first shrimp boat
constructed by Norman Bellamy

his own idea of what he wanted. Every boat was custom-built.

"And I had some plans of my own that I initiated. I put a twin loader, twin keels, in a boat. It acted as a stabilizer, keeping the boat from rolling. You could ride this boat up on the railway to launch it. You didn't need to block it, chock it, or anything. If it went aground, it would never turn over on you. You could run it right up on the beach, and the tide would leave it and the tide would take it back.

"The man who was doing the measurements out of Savannah, Georgia, had done survey work up and down the coast, and he said that he had never seen a boat like that before."

One of the twin-keel boats that he is most proud of is called the *Royal Princess*. He built it for a golf-equipment company in Chicago to cruise from the Great Lakes down the St. Lawrence River and through the Panama Canal to the west coast. Ninety-three feet long, the *Royal Princess* accommodates two hundred people. It is fitted with five wet bars, water makers, two thirty-kilowatt diesel generators, three Caterpillars, battery chargers, and refrigerators. It is a sleek, classy boat. "The original owner sold it, and it's now in Vancouver," Norman said, "running sightseeing tours along the coast. I hear from the new owner quite often. The boat recently capsized in a freak typhoon. I had six inches of styrofoam through all the inside walls and bulkheads, so it wouldn't sink but so far down. They pumped it out, washed it down, and it's as good as new."

Although he built five or six other boats in the ninety-foot class, his boats averaged sixty-five feet in length, especially the shrimp boats. Having built numerous shrimp boats, Norman observed that some people were buying old shrimpers and converting them into pleasure boats, called "shrimper's yachts." They would remove all the rigging from the shrimp boat, renovate the hull, and put a custom-built house on it. "So I designed one around that idea," Norman said, "and built a shrimper's hull and put a custom-built house on it. It was never a shrimper, though it would have the same hull. These boats sold pretty well."

Although he has not kept any written records of his boats, Norman recently acquired a camcorder and has made many hours of tapes showing some of his boats shrimping and unloading. He also has a photograph album containing numerous old pictures of his boats in various stages of construction.

His rich past, recorded in pictures and memories, however, is at odds with the current derelict state of boatbuilding and shrimping, leading him to have strong feelings about governmental regulations: "The shrimpers are blamed for killing the turtles. When I was a boy, I could go up on this beach here—there was nobody living over there—and jump from one turtle nest to another right on down the beach. No one over there was disturbing them. It was quiet, plenty of birds. Man took note of the beach and destroyed all the wildlife over there, including the turtles. They're not coming up on that beach where lights are burning, where people are at, to lay their eggs. They can't get nowhere to lay, and they spawn right in the water, where the fish eat the eggs. Over at Bald Head Island, there are deer, rabbits, birds, and turtles. That's the last breeding place they have.

"As far as the government is concerned, however, the shrimpers are destroying the turtles. The TEDs that let the turtles out let one-third of our catch out at the same time. We're having to pay the bill to buy the TEDs. We have to take the loss. Then the government says you've got to have an apron. It's a $1,600 device you fasten onto your boat, and if the boat sinks, the device floats off and signals the Coast Guard where you are. That device wouldn't cost $200. I figure that some top officials and the company lobbyists and a few politicians got together and devised a scheme to make a lot of money.

"I'm not against safety, but there's no end of regulations. You've got to put lifesaving equipment on your boat — a lifeboat, flares. And you've got to take lessons in CPR before they allow you to buy a license for your boat.

"Then the fuel goes sky-high. Right now, it's $250 a week extra — right out of my profit, which I don't hardly even have. They add more stuff on shrimpers and run him out of business. That ain't good enough, the Pleasure Island Fishing Club got so big and strong that they control the east coast now, and they control the marine resources who used to protect commercial fishermen. They're enacting laws now into the commercial fishing industry that you can't run a net within a half-mile of the beach and that you can't run gill nets inside. So they're putting the commercial fishermen out of business. You'll have to get shrimp from Japan or South America, because the government is running their own people out of business. And nobody cares, not even these people on this beach who eat the shrimp. They don't even take the time to care. And the tourists don't realize that a way of life here is being threatened."

Norman is a man of strong opinions who, in another life, might have been a powerful political leader looking after the rights of the little man. His memories of the Great Depression and the building of the Intracoastal Waterway during that period are cases in point: "Under President Hoover, they were digging what they called 'the inside right' for the rich men that owned yachts who wanted to go to Florida without having to go the sea route. At the expense of the taxpayer. And during the time they were dredging that Waterway in 1930 and 1932, there were people in Wilmington literally starving to death. And President Hoover was building the rich man 'the inside right' to Florida.

"During the Depression, the people that farmed or fished did all right. They didn't suffer. But people in the cities, their jobs were gone and they had nothing to eat. At that time, the Waterway had no commercial value whatsoever. Those boys were digging down there twelve hours a day for twenty dollars a month. People would sit right there hoping some of them would quit so that they could take their jobs."

Although Norman never got to finish high school, he has proved himself to be an articulate, successful businessman, as well as one of the area's outstanding boatbuilders. Despite his lack of formal education, he is also an exceptional teacher. He maintains a net shop at Brunswick Community College and has taught net making during the past fifteen years. Many of the people he taught, including Ed Robinson, have gone on to open net shops on their own.

"I taught most of the fishermen around here how to make nets," Norman said. "Some, I couldn't teach. It simply wouldn't sink in. The hardest thing to do is to teach a left-handed person to make a net. I happen to be able to work with either hand. If you teach a left-handed person, you got to teach them left-handed. I say that you're never going to be able to make it in this world unless you learn to work with both hands. There's a left-handed corner and a right-handed corner on everything. If you ain't able to nail in one corner, I say you're in trouble. One fellow said, 'Well, I could turn upside down, you know, with head hanging down, and nail it.'"

Norman stopped building boats in the mid-1970s. The last boats he built were two shrimpers named the *Capt. N. C.* and the *Capt. N. C. II*, which, appropriately, bear the initials of his first and middle names: Norman Curtis. Several of his boats still work the Carolina coast, and others can be found in Rhode Island, Maine, Maryland, Key West, Fort Lauderdale, Miami, and the Gulf. Pete Singletary, who has great respect for Norman, observed that "Mr. Norman has only two faults: he's a die-hard Democrat, and he's a Caterpillar man. He always encouraged a person to buy a Caterpillar engine. We call him a Catdemocrat."

In 1983, Norman became a Baptist minister. He has baptized many people in the Cape Fear River and Lockwoods Folly River. Besides constructing several homes in the area and a hotel in nearby Bolivia, he has built several churches. Like Weston Varnam, Norman's life as a waterman and carpenter has led him to preach the gospel of the biblical carpenter and fisher of men.

A widower with five grown daughters, Norman was remarried in September 1992. He and his new wife, Almeda, were married by Ed Robinson, a skillful net maker who has also mastered the art of tying the wedding knot.

THE ARTISTIC WATERMAN

Painting by
Bryan Varnam

Although many of the natives of Varnamtown and vicinity have not had the benefit of an extended formal education, they possess a creative energy and powerful work ethic that are embodied in the hundreds of boats they have built and in the independent livelihoods they have maintained over the century. Practical men, they have never thought of the boats they shaped with an artist's eye for symmetry and balance as works of art. They are simply shrimp boats, designed for catching shrimp. Nevertheless, these practical vessels are striking artistic creations that reflect the unique talents of each builder. A powerful imagination and long years of apprenticeship are required to turn a stack of cypress and pine into a sleek craft capable of trawling through the Atlantic for thirty or forty years.

The creative spirit of the Varnam family has also manifested itself in the paintings of Bryan Varnam, the son of Ed Varnam, one of the boatbuilders who helped to shape the character of Varnamtown. We first met Bryan at the Day at the Docks celebration in March of 1992. He was exhibiting his paintings, as were several other local artists. A few days later, we visited him at his home.

Much like his uncle Weston's house, which is identified by a model shrimp boat over the driveway, Bryan's house is marked by an artist's palette attached to his mailbox. A modest house set back from the street against a woods, and with a chicken coop to one side, the place serves both as his home and studio.

A soft-spoken man in his thirties, Bryan discussed his childhood: "I was born and raised in Varnamtown. My parents' house is next door. During the summer breaks from school, I would work on building shrimp boats with my dad down at Uncle Clyde's place. We built two boats — the *Marsh Hen* and the *Daylight*. My father and Uncle Weston owned Varnam Brothers' Seafood down at Old Ferry Road when I was about ten or eleven years old. I helped pack out shrimp, head shrimp, and all that. We had our own little boat, and my father and I shrimped in the Cape Fear River and some of the tributaries.

I shrimped with him for five years. It was a lot of fun, very interesting. It was also a lot of hard work and not much money. Then I got sick and decided to get off the boat. I was painting some even back then, but after I left the boat, I didn't know anything else, so I decided to work on my painting. I got rehabilitated and evolved into an artist."

Bryan then stated something that struck us as especially perceptive. "I never knew I could *be* an artist. Around here, this is country. We never knew any artists around here. Besides," he went on, "I was sick, and people didn't think I was going to live long anyhow, so they didn't think too much about my painting then."

With no opportunity for formal training, and living in a community with little leisure and less money, it seemed almost impossible for Bryan to declare himself to be an artist. The very idea of transforming the workaday small world around him into *objets d'art* was almost unthinkable. Fortunately, however, he had a cousin living in Louisiana named Sandy Fisher who was an artist, and he became Bryan's much-needed role model.

"I did my first painting for Uncle Weston," he recalled. "A painting of one of his boats. I gave it to him, and he came back and gave me $20 for it. The last painting I sold went for $2,000. My sickness was sort of a blessing. I'm over the illness, and now I'm an artist," he smiled.

"I started painting shrimp boats, road scenes, and backwater scenes. I used to paint with oils, but now I use acrylics. Sandy uses acrylics—they dry so much faster. I've done some murals on sheetrock for local businesses. I show my work at the Festival by the Sea and at the Oyster Festival, but only at those two. The other shows are too competitive, with too many people selling too many things. I stay at home and do my thing. If I make it, I make it. If I don't, then I don't."

While many of his paintings are done on commission, Bryan acknowledges that paintings of people's houses or of local bridges are not "the most artistic things in the world, but you've still got to make a living." His modesty, however, belies a major talent. Many of his paintings of local scenes, like the one of the old Holden Beach drawbridge that used to connect the island to the mainland, or the one of the now-eroded golden dunes of the strand framing a distant trawler, evoke a powerful nostalgia through their photographic realism. His paintings of the current scene, on the other hand, such as the one of the huge new concrete bridge spanning the Intracoastal Waterway to Holden Beach, chronicle the area's transformations. Interesting details from the past, however, continue to assert themselves. In the painting of the new bridge, Norman Bellamy's trawler, *Capt. N. C. II*, occupies the foreground as it moves towards the great bridge in the distance, while a heron sits undisturbed in the shadow of the marsh grasses that fill the left corner of the foreground.

Bryan's favorite paintings are those with a nostalgic and romantic cast, quiet scenes of the backwater and mysterious roads. Two such paintings, *Backwaters I* and *Backwaters II*, for example, forsake the recognizable local area for silent, unpeopled scenes.

The former painting depicts a tin-roofed shack on the edge of still water. A rowboat is moored in front of the darkened shack. Two great trees draped with Spanish moss stand clear in the foreground against a pale mist haunting a background of vague trees.

Less forlorn, perhaps, *Backwaters II* allows some bright sky to enter the upper right side of the scene, but the focus is clearly upon a solitary rowboat moored mysteriously within a marsh. The left side of the painting is heavily weighted by a dead tree, dark green foliage, and shadows that stand in contrast to the faint light reflected off the boat's gunnels.

Despite the serenity of both paintings, they manage to convey a quiet melancholy and mystery. Who inhabits the lonely, unlighted shack by the still water, and who has left his boat tethered in the darkening marsh? The images for these paintings were not drawn from life. Rather, they are an amalgam of places Bryan has seen and, more importantly,

Bryan
Varnam

imagined. They appear to embody his romantic vision of a pristine world, secure, calm, and seductive.

Like his father and his uncles, Bryan recalls the unspoiled days of his childhood, before the real-estate agents and the tourists arrived. "People who were around when everything started to come together, they remember when the pace was very slow. People who see these old bridges and ferries," he said, referring to his paintings, "they talk about the times when you went across the ferry to the island and had to put a board in the sand to get the cars off. The only way to get up and down the strand was when it was low water and the sand was hard enough to support a car, and you got to the end of the island to where your house was, if you had one. There's a certain quality there. No longer. There are hundreds of houses over there now, with people trying to see how much money they can make on rentals. The quality of life is not near as good as it used to be."

Bryan's paintings of the small world he never imagined capable of artistic rendering now hang in homes around the nation, from California to Louisiana. Several of his works have also been carried back by visitors from England. He has also done a number of large murals, including one that wraps around the living room of his uncle Weston's house and another that graces the clubhouse of the Ocean Isle Golf Club. His days as a shrimper continue to be reflected in many of his works. One remarkable painting shows a small shrimp boat under an ominous blue-black sky heading towards a distant lighthouse. At Christmas of 1991, he completed a large acrylic for Norman Bellamy that depicts two of the trawlers that he built, the *Capt. N. C.* and the *Capt. N. C. II*, tied up at his dock.

Bryan and his wife, Tami, have two children, Brandon and Elizabeth. Reflecting on his own childhood, Bryan noted that his son was growing up in a completely different world: "Of course, he doesn't know anything about the fishing industry — packing out shrimp at twelve or one o'clock at night, being so tired, your hands cold because there's ice mixed in the shrimp, and your fingers are in there and they get pricked by the shrimp heads, and then they're so cold. He doesn't know anything about that. When I was sixteen years old, I was once so tired that I went out and lay down in the car and fell asleep instantly and woke up in somebody else's car. I was told that I was out and running around in my sleep because I was so exhausted. He knows nothing about all that. Fortunately for him, he has my father, who takes him down the river. So he knows something about the river. But unless we have some way of stopping the pollution of that river, he may not know that much longer. The runoff waters from the businesses and golf courses pollute that river after a big rain."

Bryan and Tami enjoy reading and listening to good music. Their living room is filled with bookshelves containing a wide range of books. In addition to attending to the extraordinary needs of Elizabeth, a special child, Tami manages to find time to write short stories. By working at home, Bryan is also able to help take care of the children. Both Bryan and Tami share the characteristic independence of the older Varnams, but their reading has helped sharpen their understanding of their community and the dangers that threaten it.

Bryan compared the folk in Varnamtown to those in John Steinbeck's *Cannery Row*: "The people in Varnamtown are really independent and private. They like to do their own thing—clamming, oystering, working on their boats. They are very independent, very proud, and very hard-working. The real-estate people are the ones with money, the ones who have political clout and get things done. The people who live here all their lives and make a living off the rivers and farms, they usually catch the brunt of the politics."

Tami, who had been sitting quietly during our entire interview with Bryan, at this point could no longer contain herself and spoke out: "The politicians and land offices would love to see everyone out of Varnamtown. They desperately want to put a bridge down in Varnamtown, which would totally destroy the wetlands, and connect the golf course on either side of the river to Varnamtown. One land developer said, 'These people are living on too-expensive real estate—so drive them out!' They would love to raise the property tax so high as to drive the people out. They want to outlaw commercial fishing and make it just sportfishing. When you are poor and breaking your back trying to make a living and someone waves $200,000 or $300,000 under your nose for your little piece of waterfront property, what are you to do? If you wave a few million dollars at someone who owns some woods that they have to pay outrageous property taxes on, he'll take it. That's how the golf course got built down here."

Tami spoke these words with a passion and critical intelligence that suggested she had thought long and hard about the subject. Her analysis of how the monied real-estate interests drive the natives off their inherited land struck us as being right on target. Wealthy retirement communities, golf courses, and "plantations" have already driven thousands of people off their coastal lands in Georgia, South Carolina, and North Carolina. The irony of the situation is that the very atmosphere that people are seeking in moving to these regions is being displaced by typical upscale suburban communities. Tami is keenly sensitive to the irony, and we can only hope that her articulate and critical voice will be heeded before it is too late.

Now that Varnamtown is incorporated, however, the community is changing. Tami told us that she had already been approached by someone who found her chickens "highly offensive" and asked her to get rid of them. "Now they're talking about zoning and mandatory trash collection," she said. "We have 5 aldermen for 270 people! You'd think we were a pretty rowdy bunch. So they're naming streets and giving us house numbers. That's all right, but I hope that's as far as it goes. If they try to make our town like every other small town in America, we are lost."

SMUGGLING

*T*he coast of North Carolina has been a pirate's and smuggler's paradise ever since the days of Edward Teach, better known as Blackbeard the Pirate. A daring and murderous plunderer, Blackbeard ruled the dangerous waters off the North Carolina coast and soon extended his sway over the many rivers, inlets, and sounds of the state that harbored his ships and their hidden treasures. Pardoned by royal proclamation, Blackbeard became a folk hero among the colonists when he arrived in North Carolina in 1718.

During the next two centuries, writers and later filmmakers turned this ruthless buccaneer into a figure of myth and romance. Legend has it that to this day, strange sights and sounds are heard along the Carolina coast that may be attributed to Blackbeard's headless ghost, which supposedly carries a lantern while seeking his head, severed at the battle of Ocracoke Inlet. The historian Robert E. Lee observes that "it is common on the seacoast to identify any unexplainable light as simply 'Teach's light.' Some have seen it by both land and sea, on board ghostly ships, and even moving about houses along the sandy shores."[1]

Smuggling as a way of life in the Carolinas has continued into the present time, but the booty has shifted from gold, silver, and property to illegal drugs. The present-day smugglers, however, do not share the romantic aura of their predecessors. Rather, they are viewed simply as criminals who have been indicted by federal grand juries and imprisoned. Brunswick County, with busy fishing centers in Southport and Holden Beach, became known as the drug "Gateway to the Carolinas" during the 1980s. Boats like the *Lady Ellen*, a seventy-foot trawler, and the *Amy T*, a forty-eight-foot trawler, built for the hard work of hauling in shrimp, were employed by smugglers to carry tons of marijuana and other drugs into Brunswick County from the south. A smuggler could make more money bringing in several boatloads of grass than a shrimper could earn all season long doing hard, honest work.

Between 1979 and 1983, customs agents seized forty-one vessels, five aircraft, and fifty-five vehicles involved in smuggling drugs into Brunswick County. The disclosure of this elaborate smuggling operation in the local newspapers startled the peaceful small communities of Holden Beach and Shallotte. Little did vacationers realize that several of the boats they saw

---

[1]Robert E. Lee, *Blackbeard the Pirate* (Winston-Salem, N. C.: John F. Blair, Publisher, 1976), 174.

drifting past their beach homes were not bringing in their shrimp dinners, but rather tons of illegal drugs.

An FBI sting operation in Columbus County led the government to extend its investigation into Brunswick County. The first sign of trouble there came with the discovery that three trawlers — *Hurricane David*, *Captain's Choice*, and *Captain Tom* — had carried a million dollars' worth of marijuana into Brunswick County. A careful observer walking at night along the sands of Holden Beach during March of 1980 might have seen a few small lights a mile or two out on the ocean coming towards the shore and concluded that he was witnessing the restless ghost of Edward Teach searching for his severed head. Indeed, Teach's spirit was there in the person of a North Carolina smuggler we shall call "Mr. Grass," who arranged for several small boats to ferry over eighteen tons of marijuana to shore from the abandoned fishing vessel *Captain Tom*.

All of the principals involved in this smuggling operation except for Mr. Grass were from outside of the Carolinas. A federal grand jury using the code name Operation Gateway then began investigating the extent of the smuggling operation in Brunswick County. As the grand jury proceeded with its investigation, what at first seemed to be a small operation turned out to be an elaborate drug-smuggling ring that involved high-ranking government officials.

Mr. Grass, a local shrimper and boatbuilder who was thoroughly familiar with the waters between North Carolina and Florida, masterminded the entire operation. For a period of about four years, he commanded a fleet of trawlers that regularly transported marijuana into the county. Furthermore, he managed to involve the necessary support of several important local officials in his operation.

Customs agents, alerted to his smuggling, quickly moved in to intercept his illegal cargo. In 1979, the _Pathfinder_ was seized with 16,000 pounds of marijuana. An unnamed boat attempted to smuggle in another 60,000 pounds that same year, followed by the _Queen May_ with 31,000 pounds. In 1980, the _Billy-G_ and the _Miss Mickey_ were captured in the Waterway at Holden Beach with 12,000 pounds of marijuana in their holds. That same year, 36,500 pounds of marijuana in the _Captain Tom_ were confiscated off Holden Beach. In 1981, the _Captain Jerry_ was seized with 38,000 pounds of marijuana. In addition to the confiscation of tons of marijuana, government officials also seized thousands of methaqualone tablets. The street value of the seized drugs amounted to over $180 million.

Mr. Grass pleaded guilty to smuggling operations involving the vessels _Pathfinder_, _Rusty_, _Queen Elizabeth_, _Miss Mickey_, _Billy-G_, _Captain Jerry_, and _Captain Tom_, along with three aircraft. He was given a ten-year sentence to run concurrently with a ten-year sentence he was already serving in South Carolina at the time of his trial. A total of twenty-one men were indicted on charges of drug-smuggling conspiracy, including a former Holden Beach police commissioner, a former North Carolina Fisheries official, the sheriff of Brunswick County, a former chairman of the Brunswick County Board of Commissioners who was later an official with the North Carolina Department of Transportation, and the chief of the Shallotte Police Department. The stiffest sentence, fourteen years, was given to the sheriff of Brunswick County.

After an early release from prison, Mr. Grass purchased a seafood restaurant near Holden Beach. We met him briefly one evening while dining there. An outgoing, self-confident fellow, he showed us two model shrimp boats he had constructed and placed in glass showcases in his restaurant. They were remarkably artistic replicas of the actual full-sized shrimp boats he had built for himself and which he runs to this day. A small man with an unmistakable talent and energy for manipulating the world around him, Mr. Grass has since sold his restaurant and returned to a life of occasional shrimping. An ominous scar on his cheek, however, recalls a darker, more mysterious past.

The confiscated shrimp boats used in the smuggling operation were among the innocent victims left in the wreckage of this scandal. The *Amy T*, for example, a forty-eight-foot trawler seized in 1981 by federal agents for its role in smuggling marijuana, was ravaged by weather and vandals as she sat dockside for over a year on the Cape Fear River in Wilmington. Like the other confiscated vessels, she was put up for auction in 1983 by the United States Customs Agency. Some fishermen believe that customs agents hide a very sensitive electronic bug on the confiscated vessels so that they can maintain constant surveillance of their auctioned boats. Federal officials deny this.

In any event, a man by the name of Bill Stanley came to Wilmington to bid on the *Amy T*, which had been taken from the former Holden Beach police commissioner, who denied it was used for smuggling. Stanley hoped to restore her to good health and service. After winning the *Amy T* with a bid of $13,000, he said, "Her reputation's bad now. Her name is tarnished. But she will shine again and hold her head up with pride."[2]

Confiscated drug-smuggling boats have not only been refurbished to shine again, but some of them have been instrumental in developing the sportfishing business. With the cooperation of the North Carolina Division of Marine Fisheries, the Long Bay Artificial Reef Association, established in 1984, has built six artificial reefs: two off Lockwoods Folly Inlet, two off Shallotte Inlet, and two off the Cape Fear River. In the summer of 1991, the 170-foot Panamanian drug boat *Jell II*, seized off the Brunswick County coast in the early 1980s, was sunk about ten miles off Lockwoods Folly Inlet. By the fall, small fish had begun to feed on the soft corals and other organisms that attached themselves to the sunken vessel. These fish, in turn, lured larger predators, such as king mackerel, to the area, providing fishermen with a rich harvest. Little did the smugglers of the 1980s suspect that their furtive boats, accustomed to the night, would one day brighten the days of Brunswick fishermen.

None of the boats built by the Varnam family or by Norman Bellamy was involved in these scandals. A man who owned one of Billy Varnam's boats, however, was charged with possession of marijuana, but he went to court and was found not guilty. Overjoyed by the verdict, he named his boat *Not Guilty* to proclaim and memorialize his innocence throughout Brunswick County and points south.

---

[2]The *Brunswick Beacon* (February 17, 1983), 7.

CONNECTIONS

*T*here are numerous interlocking connections in the small area of Brunswick County explored in this book. Four generations of the Varnam family, with an initial connection to Maine, have lived together near Holden Beach in a town now bearing their name. Weston, Clyde, Ed, Hoyal, and Billy Varnam are linked to Norman Bellamy through their shared years of boatbuilding. These men, in turn, have close ties with Danny Galloway, William Varnam, Henderson and Charlie Caison, and many other shrimpers who earn their living off the locally built boats. The fishermen, then, depend upon people like Pete Singletary, Freddie Fulford, and Wycuff Skipper to sell their catch. Finally, the visitors to Holden Beach and some of the area residents purchase the shrimp and fish either in local restaurants or at fish houses.

This cycle of connections, however, has grown more complicated in recent years. The building of shrimp boats has passed from the scene. The shrimpers, meanwhile, do their best to maintain their boats but find themselves with new and more demanding connections than they experienced in the past: connections with federal and state agencies that continue to tighten regulations on shrimping, connections with sportfishermen who want more of the ocean for themselves, and connections with environmentalists seeking to restrict the shrimpers' harvest. The increasing importation of foreign shrimp cultivated in ponds threatens to remove the Carolina watermen from the cycle altogether.

There are also important physical connections to be noted: the new, imposing bridge connecting Holden Beach to the mainland, the improved paved roads leading to the tidy subdivisions and golf-club estates springing up in the area. People from around the country are retiring to the coastal Carolinas in record numbers, and thousands of visitors come every year to rent homes on and near the beaches. This major relocation of people is, perhaps, the most dangerous of all connections for the Carolina watermen.

People like Weston Varnam and Norman Bellamy, recalling their boyhood memories, can still picture Holden Beach as an area of golden sand and tall dunes where they could go to fish or hunt for turtle eggs. The development of Holden Beach, however, has brought about some ironic changes in their lives.

The influx of visitors over the years helped to create a market for fresh fish and shrimp, thereby spurring the growth of the boatbuilding and fishing industries. But as the development continued, there gradually arose two distinct worlds, that of the watermen and that of the visitors. The only real connection between them was a monetary one. The visitors enjoyed eating fresh seafood during their vacations. So far, so good.

These same visitors, however, with the helpful guidance of realtors and land developers, began to settle in the area, lured by the small-town, slow-paced, rustic charm of the coastal scene. In order to accommodate the demand for retirement communities, numerous upper-middle-class suburbs, some built around sprawling golf courses, were built in the area. The very charm of the rough-edged Southern town that first captivated these newcomers has now been largely displaced by manicured, professional landscapes fleshed out with homes costing upwards of $200,000.

As we drove through the expensive suburb called Riverside, located at the edge of Lockwoods Folly River, we recalled Clyde Varnam's memory of that place when it was called Wild Cat. It was there that Clyde worked on his first boat — the last one built by his father — which caught fire one night. "The fire burned the side of an old white oak," he remembered. "In fact, it's still standing down there." We thought about the residents of Riverside who might have wondered how that tree became scarred but who do not realize that the white oak stands today in the mind of an old boatbuilder as his vital connection with his father.

Small communities such as Varnamtown that have existed

for nearly a century are connected by a complex web of memories, family relationships, friendships, and a shared experience of living off the rivers and ocean. Their neighborhoods are like extended families. Fathers, sons, daughters, and grandchildren live in homes within shouting distance of each other. The business of running the fish houses and shrimp boats is passed from one generation to another. These people believe in the old-fashioned values of hard work and independence. Mostly Baptists, they live by strict religious codes. Weston Varnam and Norman Bellamy have enriched their communities not only through their boatbuilding, but also through their preaching at the local churches. None of the people we interviewed smoked or drank alcohol, contrary to the stereotypical image of the swaggering, hard-living fisherman.

Despite the fundamental American values embodied in these people, their way of life is seriously threatened by the increasing number of outsiders moving into their area. Like the loggerheads, they are an endangered species. Their land is now more valuable than ever, and as the tax rate continues to rise, developers will put even greater pressure on them to sell, so that new suburbs and golf courses may be built. The delicate shrimp boat balanced over Weston Varnam's driveway and the artist's palette hanging on Bryan Varnam's mailbox may not endure. As Tami Varnam said, "If they try to make our town like every other small town in America, we are lost."

Many of the important connections examined in this small book are those of the mind — the powerful links between the past and the present and the ambiguous links between the present and the future. Holden Beach, Riverside, and the golfing communities have buried some of the region's past. The fragments of the Carolina watermen's history, however, still shine through in Varnamtown, in the old wooden shrimp boats, and in the minds and hearts of the men who built and run them.

Finally, there is our own connection with the people and places in this book. When we first came to Holden Beach, our vision was limited to our beach house, the sand, and the water. Holden Beach was a place where we tried to forget the problems of the world and relax. Instead of watching television, we watched the distant, mysterious shrimp boats slowly moving past our house. In wondering about what the people on those boats were doing and thinking, we soon found ourselves entering a new world, one peopled with the fascinating individuals who make up this book. Many of the watermen we talked to have not been on Holden Beach for decades. It has become an alien place to them, especially during the summer, filled with people they do not know or understand. We, too, are among those alien visitors, but we have been fortunate in making some memorable connections with the Carolina watermen, their friends and families, their proud history and uncertain future.

Brunswick County Shrimp Landings

	Fish	Pounds	Value
1983	Brown shrimp	566,074	$1,190,715
	Pink shrimp	7,532	$21,792
	White shrimp	190,627	$522,287
1984	Brown shrimp	690,722	$1,341,347
	Pink shrimp	12,770	$36,321
	White shrimp	39,269	$103,876
1985	Brown shrimp	209,314	$321,940
	Pink shrimp	299	$320
	White shrimp	10,244	$24,057
1986	Brown shrimp	202,966	$325,995
	Pink shrimp	14,362	$40,194
	Rock shrimp	37	$67
	White shrimp	48,311	$120,729
1987	Brown shrimp	152,173	$260,779
	Pink shrimp	2,123	$6,781
	White shrimp	79,691	$169,382
1988	Brown shrimp	303,600	$516,134
	Pink shrimp	6,560	$20,043
	Rock shrimp	62	$70
	White shrimp	6,942	$22,802
1989	Brown shrimp	320,508	$416,260
	Pink shrimp	22,058	$61,783
	White shrimp	291,010	$585,577

	Fish	Pounds	Value
1990	Brown shrimp	387,481	$649,482
	Pink shrimp	7,733	$23,274
	White shrimp	204,011	$526,432
1991	Brown shrimp	295,699	$412,857
	White shrimp	239,699	$430,663
1992	Brown shrimp	247,164	$397,321
	White shrimp	280,486	$619,570

Boats Built by Billy Varnam

Month/Year	Name	Length	Width	Depth
8/66	S. W. J.	51-10	17	4-4
1/67	Jeanie Marie	64	19	4-11
3/67	Comanche	55-5	17	4-6
6/67	Albatross	54-11	17	4-3
9/67	Miss Evans	67-2	19	5-4
1/68	Billy Boy	43-2	13	3-6
3/68	Miss Kim	56-2	17	4-7
6/68	Chris	56-4	17	4-7
9/68	Molly Ray	64-6	21	5-6
1/69	Papa Lloyd	67-8	21	5-7
3/69	Octopus	68-5	21	5-8
6/69	Squid	70-10	21	6-5
9/69	Black Fish	35-7	12	3-4
1/70	Lauraanne	55-3	17	4-5
3/70	River Boy	60-9	17	4-6
6/70	Drag Net	62-7	20	4-10
3/71	Lady Phyllis	88-5	25	7
5/71	Scraps	53-6	17	4-1
10/71	Libby Robbie	72-3	21	5-8
3/72	Sea Dragon	67-3	21	5-4
4/72	Billy Boy II	49	16	3-9
6/72	Lucky Three	83-11	26	5-11
12/72	Phillip Marshall	78-7	23	5-6

Month/Year	Name	Length	Width	Depth
6/73	*Sundown*	66-10	21	5
12/73	*Miss Aylor*	71-9	23	5-11
7/74	*Walter Daphne*	85	25	6-5
2/75	*Preacher Boy*	69-2	19	6-2
5/76	*Capt. Ross*	72-5	20	6-2
12/76	*Capt. Earl*	80-9	23	7
9/77	*Capt. Leonard*	80-8	23	8
6/78	*Capt. Shannon*	82-5	23	8
10/78	*Capt. Chance*	82-10	23	7-6
4/79	*Capt. Elroy*	84-2	23	7-11
3/80	*Farmer's Daughter*	91-5	23	8-4
8/80	*Big Mama*	96	24	8-5
5/81	*Miss Marie*	69-6	23	6
7/83	*Not Guilty*	44	16	4
4/84	*Capt. David*	82	22	7-11
6/87	*Judy Ann*	46	15	4
4/89	*P & N I*	40	13-8	4-8
5/89	*P & N II*	40	13-8	4-8
5/89	*Windjammer*	61-2	19-4	5-5
6/91	*Predator*	43	14	5

INDEX